SHIPS FROM IRELAND TO EARLY AMERICA, 1623 - 1850

Volume IV

by
David Dobson

Copyright © 2018
by David Dobson
All Rights Reserved

Printed for Clearfield Company by
Genealogical Publishing Company
Baltimore, Maryland
2018

ISBN 9780806358710

INTRODUCTION

A major hurdle experienced by many family historians in North America is making the link back across the Atlantic to Europe. This is especially true for the United States before 1820, when the recording of immigrants became compulsory. Canadian genealogists have an even more difficult task, as only after Confederation in 1865 was the recordkeeping of immigrants introduced. (In 1828, the British Government ordered that manifests listing passengers be kept by shipmasters; some of these have survived in Canadian archives.

During the seventeenth, eighteenth, and early nineteenth centuries, many emigrants travelled as cabin or steerage passengers aboard merchant vessels designed to transport cargoes, thus conditions aboard ship were relatively primitive. In 1803 the British Government passed Ship Passengers Acts which improved the ratio between the ship's tonnage and the maximum number of passengers carried. This reduced the volume of emigration aboard British ships. Subsequent U.S. legislation was tougher than the contemporary British laws; this in practice caused a diversion of the emigrant trade from the British Isles to Canadian ports. Many Irish landing at Canadian ports, such as Halifax, ultimately moved south to the United States.

This book is designed as an aid to family historians in North America researching their Irish ancestry. It identifies vessels from Ireland known to, or likely to, have been carrying passengers. Sometimes the port of embarkation may indicate the district in Ireland that the emigrants originated from. The volume of ships bound from Ireland to the Caribbean also suggests a two-stage migration pattern – with immigrants firstly arriving as indentured servants to the West Indies, followed by their movement to the mainland colonies. From the mid seventeenth century onwards, Ireland had a significant trade, especially in beef, dairy produce, and linen, with the English colonies in the West Indies, and such trading links facilitated emigration. At the same time the transportation of rebels and felons created sizable Irish communities in the Caribbean, such as in Montserrat. In due course there was migration from the West Indies north to the Carolinas and other British colonies in America. Most ships leaving Ireland bound for the Americas--following the winds and currents--sailed south to Madeira or the Azores, then crossed to the West Indies, and from there headed north to the American colonies. Vessels bound for the Canadian Maritimes and New England, however, crossed directly.

This is the fourth and final volume in the series *'Ships from Ireland to Early America, 123-1850'*. It is based on both primary and secondary, manuscript and published sources in North America, Madeira, Britain and especially Ireland.

David Dobson

Dundee, Scotland

June 2018

SHIPS FROM IRELAND TO EARLY AMERICA, 1623-1850, IV

REFERENCES

ActsPCCol		Acts of the Privy Council, Colonial
ARM	=	Madeira Regional Archives
BJ	=	Bristol Journal, series
BNL	=	Belfast Newsletter, series
CBC	=	Council Book of the Corporation of Cork
CM	=	Caledonian Mercury, series
DI	=	Dublin Intelligencer, series
DNL	=	Dublin News Letter, series
DWJ	=	Dublin Weekly Journal, series
FDJ	=	Faulkner's Dublin Journal, series
FLJ	=	Finn's Leinster Journal, series
Harl.	=	Harley ms, British Museum
IC	=	Ireland under the Commonwealth, [Manchester, 1913]
LJ	=	Londonderry Journal, series
LL	=	Lloyd's Lists, series
LRS	=	London Record Society
PCCol	=	Acts of the Privy Council, Colonial
QG	=	Quebec Gazette, series
SM	=	Scots Magazine, series
SPAWI	=	Cal. State Papers, America West Indies
SNL	=	Saunders Newsletter, series

SHIPS FROM IRELAND TO EARLY AMERICA, 1623-1850, IV

W   =   Waterford, History & Society
          [Dublin, 1992]

WI   =   Without Indentures,
          [Rochester, New York, 2013]

SHIPS FROM IRELAND TO EARLY AMERICA, 1623-1850, IV

ABB, Captain Brownrigg, from Cork to Grenada in 1772. [LL.3741]

ABBY PRATT, arrived in New York *with passengers* from Ireland on 25 August 1849. [IHR.39.156]

ABERDEEN, arrived in New York *with passengers* from Ireland on 13 March 1850. [IHR.39.156]

ABRAHAM, supercargo Thomas Anthony, from Cork, Bandon, and Youghal, *with forty-one male and twenty female indentured servants* bound for Barbados in November 1637. [TNA.HCA.Misc. bundle 30.636]

ABRAHAM, master James Rivett, from London via Glasgow and Belfast to Madeira and Nevis, *with passengers,* 1679; master Abraham Terry, from Chester via Cork to the West Indies in 1680, *with passengers*; master Abraham Terry, from London via Waterford to Nevis, 1681. [LRS.36.117/118/163/222]

ABRAHAM, Captain Copeland, from Dublin to Grenada on 31 December 1765. [LL.3128]

ACTIVE, Captain Staunton, from Cork to Jamaica on 7 January 1766. [LL.3131]

ACTIVE, Captain Staunton, from Dublin to Antigua in 1799. [LL.3068]

ACTIVE, Captain Betty, arrived in St Vincent in May 1803 from Cork. [LL.4356]; master Thomas Faed, at Funchal, Madeira, 16 December 1807 bound from Cork to Haiti with 2 passengers. [ARM.ms600; CM.Funchal.696]

ACTIVE, Captain Johnson, arrived in Quebec on 30 July 1823 from Newry. [LL.5836]

SHIPS FROM IRELAND TO EARLY AMERICA, 1623-1850, IV

ACTRESS, from Cork to New York, arrived on 1 December 1818. [LL.5348]

ADALINE, arrived in New York *with passengers* from Ireland on 8 June 1850. [IHR.39.156]

ADMIRAL KEPPEL, Captain Copplestone, from Cork to Jamaica, 26 December 1773. [LL.500]

ADVENTURE OF HULL, master Lancelot Anderson, from Kinsale to Maryland, in 1666. [ActsPCCol.1667.722]

ADVENTURE, master ..... Washington, from Cork bound for Jamaica, captured by the French and taken to Port au Prince in 1758. [SM.20.330]

ADVENTURE, from Alexandria, Virginia, to Ireland, and return in 1769. [BNL.March 1769]

ADVENTURE, Captain McHucheon, arrived in Jamaica on 16 January 1826 from Belfast. [LL.6105]

ADVICE, Captain Owens, from Youghal *with passengers* bound for Newfoundland in May 1780. [FLJ.24-27 May 1780]

AELUS, Captain Howland, arrived in New York on 12 June 1817 from Londonderry. [LL.5195]

AEOLUS, from Sligo *with 428 passengers* to St John, New Brunswick, landed there on 2 November 1847. [QG.5.5.1847]

AGNES, a brig, master Robert Ewing, from Belfast *with passengers* bound for Newcastle, Delaware, and Philadelphia, arrived 26 June 1773.

SHIPS FROM IRELAND TO EARLY AMERICA, 1623-1850, IV

AGNES OF BALLYSHANNON, from Ballyshannon *with passengers* bound for St John, New Brunswick, in August 1831, landed at Bedford, Maine. [Balllyshannon Herald: 6.1.1832]

AGNES AND JEAN OF AYR, from Cork via Madeira to Barbados and Antigua in 1732. [NRS.AC9.1188]

AGREEMENT OF YOUGHAL, Captain Joseph ......, from Youghal via Nevis bound for New England in 1680. [SPAWI.1689.1621]

AGUILAR, Captain Ashington, from Cork to Jamaica in May 1803. [LL.4356]

AJAX, master .... Wallace, from Boston to Waterford in 1772. [LL.3743]

ALBION, Captain Hayton, from Cork to Jamaica in 1803. [LL.4347]

ALBION, Captain Holmes, arrived in Antigua on 28 February 1819 from Dublin. [LL.5383]

ALEXANDER, master James Hunter, from Londonderry *with passengers* bound for Newcastle, Delaware, and Philadelphia, arrived there 6 August 1773.

ALEXANDER, Captain Gale, arrived in Savannah, Georgia, in 1817 from Cork. [LL.5185]

ALEXANDER, arrived in Quebec in July 1822 from Belfast. [LL.5726]; arrived in Quebec on 20 June 1823 from Belfast. [LL.5284]

ALEXIS, Captain Wilson, arrived in Wilmington in May 1803 from Newry. [LL.4355]

ALICE, a brigantine, master Peter Jackson, at Funchal, Madeira, in October 1793 when bound from Cork to Grenada. [ARM.ms699]

ALMIRA, Captain Marshall, arrived in New York in June 1803 from Limerick. [LL.4367]

AMAZON, Captain Van Horn, arrived in Baltimore, Maryland, on 14 April 1826 from Waterford. [LL.6119]; arrived in Quebec in May 1826 from Belfast. [LL.6131]

AMERICA, master .... Gemmel, from Cork bound for Guadeloupe, was captured by the French and landed in Martinique, French West Indies, in 1760. [SM.22.271]

AMERICAN EAGLE, arrived in New York on 13 May 1803 from Belfast. [LL.4360]

AMHERST, Captain Scott, from Cork to New York in 1764. [LL.2966]

AMIABLE CLARISSA, a brigantine, master James Ayer, at Funchal, Madeira, 29 December 1791 when bound from Cork to Dominica. [ARM.ms698]

AMICABLE, Captain Erickson, arrived in Philadelphia on 22 February 1819 from Cork. [LL.5372]

AMITY OF BRISTOL, at Kinsale in January 1669 bound for the West Indies. [CSPIre.1669]

AMITY, Captain Nevin, from Belfast bound for Dominica was captured by a French privateer in 1793. [SM.55.306]

AMPRIDITE, arrived in Quebec in July 1822 from Newry. [LL.5726]

AMPLION, arrived in Quebec on 31 July 1823 from Dublin. [LL.5836]

ANACREON, Captain Stonehouse, from Sligo to Quebec in 1825. [LL.6048]

ANGEL GABRIEL, master John Duttas, from Belfast (?), Ireland, to Nevis, St Kitts, and Barbados, in 1662. [PRONI.MIC.19.1]

ANN, 300 tons, master John Jones, from Bristol via Ireland bound for Jamaica and Virginia, 1707. [APCCol.1707.974]

ANN, Captain Kavish, from Cork to Tortula on 31 December 1765. [LL.3129]

ANNE OF LONDONDERRY, from Baltimore, Maryland, bound for Londonderry, 1767. [MdGaz.31 1.1767]

ANN, 100 tons, Captain Connolly, from Waterford to Newfoundland, 12 voyages, 1766-1771. [W.399]

ANNE, master Ben Edmondson, from Cork *with 300 passengers* bound for Philadelphia in 1784. [Londonderry Journal: 3.8.1784]

ANN OF LONDONDERRY, master James Ramage, from Londonderry to Philadelphia, *with 240 passengers* in December 1785. [Pennsylvania Packet: 6.12.1785]

ANNE, a brigantine, master James Nelson, at Funchal, Madeira, 8 April 1794 when bound from Dublin to Jamaica. [ARM.ms699]

ANN, Captain Ryan, arrived in Newfoundland in June 1803 from Ross. [LL.4367]

ANN, Captain Scott, arrived in New York during 1817 from Dublin. [LL.5183]

ANN, arrived in Quebec in July 1822 from Limerick. [LL.5726]

ANN OF HALIFAX, from Ireland *with passengers* bound for Canada in 1832. [PRONI.Mic.205/1]

ANN AND ELIZA, master Alexander Phoenix, from New York bound for Ireland in December 1732. [TNA.CO5.114.111]

ANN AND JAMES OF LONDONDERRY, trading to New York during the 1760s.

ANN AND MARY, arrived in Newcastle, Delaware, from Ireland, May 1742. [PaGaz]

ANN AND SARAH, master John Marshall, from Liverpool to America *with passengers* in 1697-1698. [LRO]

ANN AND ELIZABETH, from New York to Ireland and return in 1732-1733.

ANN AND MARY, from Ireland to Newcastle, Delaware, 1742. [Pa. Gaz]

ANNA, a brigantine, master Richard Barry, at Funchal, Madeira, on 10 March 1795 when bound from Dublin to the West Indies. [ARM.ms699]

ANN ALEXANDER, Captain Allen, arrived in New York on 22 February 1817 from Dublin. [LL.5161]

ANSON, Captain Westcots, arrived in Boston in May 1803 from Cork. [LL.4360]

ANTELOPE, master .... Brayley, from Waterford bound for Newfoundland, captured by the French and taken to Bayonne, France, in 1757. [SM.19.278]

ANTIGUA, Captain Wilcock, from Cork to Antigua in 1766. [LL.3173]

ANTIGUA PACKET, master Samuel Oliver, from Antigua to Dublin, 1743. [NRS.GD205.53.8]

ANTRIM, a snow, from Larne bound for New York, 1750; from Larne bound for Philadelphia and New York, 1753 and 1754. She was wrecked off the coast of Kintyre, Scotland, on a return voyage in February 1756. [BNL.12 August 1750; 10 August 1753, 19 July 1754]

ARDENT, from Londonderry *with passengers* bound for Baltimore, Maryland, in 1803. [NEHGR.LX.163]

ARETHUSA, from Belfast to New York in 1825. [LL.6048]; Captain Clements, arrived in Jamaica on 9 February 1826. [LL.6104]

ARGYLE, master ...... Clarke, from Cork bound for St Kitts, captured by the privateers of St Malo, France, in 1757. [SM.19.325]

ARGYLE, master ...... Jervois, from Cork bound for the Leeward Islands, captured by the French and taken to Martinique, French West Indies, in 1759. [SM.22.49]

ARGYLE, Captain Anderson, arrived in Quebec in May 1826 from Waterford. [LL.6131]

ARIADNE, master ..... Russell, from Cork to Dominica in 1772. [LL.3740]

ARMATA, Captain Howland, arrived in Baltimore, Maryland, on 14 April 1826 from Limerick. [LL.6119]

ARMSTRONG, master ..... Montford, from Belfast bound for Antigua, captured by the French and taken to Martinique French West Indies, in 1759. [SM.22.105]

SHIPS FROM IRELAND TO EARLY AMERICA, 1623-1850, IV

ASTON, Captain Westcutt, arrived in Boston on 14 May 1803 from Cork. [LL.4360]

ATLANTIC, a galley, master John Nunes, at Funchal, Madeira, 19 December 1793 when bound from Cork to Barbados. [ARM.ms699]

ATLANTIC, Captain Taylor, from Belfast to New York in 1825. [LL.6048]; Captain Feadick, arrived in New York on 15 December 1825. [LL.6083]; Captain Fosdick, arrived in Philadelphia on 5 April 1826 from Belfast. [LL.6114]

ATLANTIC, Captain Lawson, arrived in Quebec on 20 May 1826 from Belfast. [LL.6130]

AUCTOMEDIC, arrived in St John's, New Brunswick, in April 1826 from Cork. [LL.6120]

AURORA, Captain Peacock, from Cork to St Kitts, 21 December 1773. [LL.499]

AURORA, master James Cotter, at Funchal, Madeira, 11 October 1793 when bound from Cork to Barbados. [ARM.ms699]; Captain Thraithwaite, arrived in Antigua on 30 April 1817, [LL.5184]; Captain Watson, arrived in Barbados on 22 April 1826 from Belfast. [LL.6124]

BACCHUS, master Thomas Eaton, from Bristol and Cork bound for Jamaica, 1762. [APCCol.1762.467]

BACHELOR, master ... Walker, from Cork to Jamaica in 1772. [LL.3742]

BALL, a privateer, from Ireland, captured by the French and taken to Martinique in 1760. [SM.22.334]

BALTIMORE, Captain Hamilton, from Cork to St Kitts in 1766. [LL.3167]

SHIPS FROM IRELAND TO EARLY AMERICA, 1623-1850, IV

BARBADOS, Captain Lee, from Newry to Quebec in 1825. [LL.6048]

BATCHELOR, a ketch, from Waterford bound for Nevis, 1678. [LRS.36.45]

BEAVER, Captain Johnson, from Cork bound for Jamaica, 1762. [APCCol.1762.467]

BEAVER, Captain Anderson, arrived in St John, New Brunswick, on 22 May 1826 from Londonderry. [LL.6121]

BELFAST PACKET, from Belfast bound for Philadelphia, Pennsylvania, in February 1766; from Philadelphia bound for Belfast, May 1766, [BNL.25.2.1766][Pa.Journal; 1 May 1766]

BELLA, master .....Middleton, from Dublin bound for Virginia, captured by the French and taken to Bayonne, France, in 1757. [SM.19.278]

BELLISLE, Captain Hughson, arrived in St John, New Brunswick, on 18 May 1826 from Cork. [LL.18 May 1826. [LL.6121]

BELLONA, Captain Williams, arrived in Halifax, Nova Scotia, in 1817 from Cork. [LL.5185]

BENEFIT OF KINSALE, returned to Kinsale from Virginia on 14 June 1670. [CSPIre.]

BENJAMIN AND HANNAH OF BOSTON, a brig, from Cork *with 25 servants* bound for New York in June 1732. [TNA.CO5.114.111]; arrived in Newcastle, Delaware, and Philadelphia, Pennsylvania, *with passengers* in late 1732.

SHIPS FROM IRELAND TO EARLY AMERICA, 1623-1850, IV

BEST, a brigantine, master John Nunes at Funchal, Madeira, on 13 December 1791 and on 9 March 1793 when bound from Cork to Barbados. [ARM.mss698/699]

BETSEY, master ..... Quinlin, from Antigua bound for Limerick, captured by the French and taken to a small port near Morlaix, France, in 1756. [SM.19.53]

BETSY, 40 tons, Captain Gaffney {?}, from Waterford to Newfoundland, 1766-1771. [W.399]

BETSEY, 45 tons, Captain Shaw. From Waterford to the West Indies, 1766-1771. [W.399]

BETSEY, master David McCutcheon, from Cork *with passengers* bound for Philadelphia, Pennsylvania, arrived 27 November 1772; master David McCutcheon, from Newry *with passengers* bound for Newcastle, Delaware, and Philadelphia, arrived 8 July 1773.

BETSEY, Captain Bennett, from Dublin to St Vincent in 1802. [LL.4320]

BETSEY, Captain Terry, arrived in New York in June 1803 from Galway. [LL.4367]

BETSEY, master James Hatrick, at Funchal, Madeira, 26 January 1808, bound from Cork with *four passengers*. [ARM.ms600; CM.Funchal.596]

BETSY, master .....Shaw, from Waterford to Barbados in 1772. [LL.3742]

BETSY, arrived in Quebec in July 1822 from Londonderry. [LL.5726]

BETTY, from Belfast to New England in 1718. [Boston Newsletter: 23.6.1718]

SHIPS FROM IRELAND TO EARLY AMERICA, 1623-1850, IV

BETTY, Captain Norris, from Cork to Tortula, 21 December 1773. [LL.499]

BETTY GREGG, Captain Scott, from Dublin to Antigua in 1772. [LL.3742]

BETTY AND MARTHA, master .... Simondson, from Cork bound for Jamaica in 1758, captured by the French and taken to Cuba. [SM.20.219]

BETTY AND SALLY OF DUBLIN, master David Johnston, from Barbados to Ireland, 1753. [PRONI.*D354*/537]

BIG WOLF OF VIRGINIA, master Martin Murphy, from Hampton, Virginia, to Dublin, 1775. [SFV.213]

BLAKENEY, Captain Baker, from Dublin bound for Philadelphia, Pennsylvania, in 1759, captured by the French but later ransomed. [SM.21.50]

BLENHEIM, Captain Warre, arrived in Waterford from Newfoundland in 1825. [LL.6055]

BLESSING OF COMBE, Captain Jesep, arrived in Kinsale in August 1669 from the Leeward Islands. [CSPIre.1669]

BOLIVAR, Captain Crosby, arrived in Quebec in May 1826 from Belfast. [LL.6131]

BONDVENTURE, from Ireland to Jamaica *with 100 soldiers* was captured by a French warship in 1705. [TNA.SP44.241-249]

BORDEAUX OF FLUSHING, master Cloys Cloyson, from the West Indies bound for Waterford, was captured by a Parliamentary ship in 1647. [TNA.HCA13.62]

SHIPS FROM IRELAND TO EARLY AMERICA, 1623-1850, IV

BOWDEN. Captain Cumming, from Waterford to Newfoundland in April 1803. [LL.4350]

BOYLE, Captain Kendall, from Dublin to Virginia in 1766. [LL.3164]

BOYNE, Captain Godfrey, from Philadelphia, Pennsylvania, to Ireland in 1756. [PRONI.D354.1034]; master Samuel Cunningham, from Belfast *with passengers* bound for Newcastle, Delaware, and Philadelphia, Pennsylvania, in 1772.

BRIDGE, master ... Tower, from Philadelphia to Cork in 1772. [LL.3742]

BRIDGET, 130 tons, Captain Berill, from Waterford to Newfoundland, four voyages, 1766-1771. [W.399]

BRIDGETOWN, Captain Ramsay, from Cork to Barbados on 26 December 1773. [LL.500]

BRISK, Captain McDowell, from Newry to Quebec in 1825. [LL.6048]

BRISTOL, a galley, via Ireland bound for Barbados, 1705. [APCCol.1705.915]

BRISTOL PACKET, Captain Vesey, from Cork to St Kitts in 1766. [LL.3164]

BRISTOL, Captain Briggs, arrived in New York on 12 July 1817, from Newry. [LL.5202]

BRITANNIA, Captain Mitchell, from Waterford to Newfoundland, 14 April 1774. [LL.531]

BRITANNIA, master Richard Eyres, from Dublin *with passengers* bound for Philadelphia, Pennsylvania, arrived there on 18 May 1773.

BRITANNIA, Captain Anderson, from Dublin to New York arrived there on 1 December 1818. [LL.5348]

BRITON, Captain Scanlon, arrived in Antigua from Dublin on 20 April 1826. [LL.6121]

BROTHERS, 120 tons, Captain Wiseman, from Waterford to Newfoundland, four voyages between 1766-1771. [W.399]

BRUERTON OF LIVERPOOL, master John Fowler, from Belfast *with 32 indentured servants* bound for Philadelphia, Pennsylvania, in 1729. [PRONI.D354/477]

BRUNSWICK, a snow, from Belfast bound for Philadelphia, in 1730, 1731, 1732, 1733. [PaGaz]

BRYAN, Captain Dougall, from Dublin to Antigua in 1805. [LL.4226]

BURWELL, master .... Wilson, from Dublin to Virginia in 1756. [PRONI.D354/714]

CAESAR, master William Prince, from Liverpool, England, and Cork bound for Jamaica, 1762. [APCCol.1762.467]

CADIZ PACKET, Captain McKibben, from Belfast on 2 October 1790 bound for Antigua. [LL.2237]

CALEDONIA, Captain McComb, from Belfast to Charleston, South Carolina, in 1825. [LL.5975]

CALEDONIA, Captain Healey, arrived in Newfoundland on 20 May 1826 from Waterford. [LL.6121]

CAMBRIDGE, Captain Burgess, from Cork to New York in 1825. [LL.6048]

CAMPDEN, Captain McClelland, from Cork to Barbados in 1766. [LL.3170]

CARLISLE OF BALTIMORE, master John Taylor, arrived in Belfast in June 1767 from Baltimore, Maryland; from Belfast *with passengers* bound for Baltimore in August 1767; arrived in Belfast from Baltimore, and left *with passengers* bound for Baltimore in 1768, also in 1769. [BNL.30 June 1767; 2 August 1768; 25 July 1769]

CARLOTA, master John Moore, at Funchal, Madeira, on 11 October 1793 when bound from Cork to Antigua. [ARM.ms699]

CAROL ANN, Captain Beach, arrived in Philadelphia on 5 April 1826 from Belfast. [LL.6114]

CASTOR, Captain Sims, from Virginia to Dublin in 1793. [LL.2470]

CATHARINE OF WORKINGTON, a 110 ton snow, master Robert Walker, from Portrush, Ireland, *with 202 passengers* bound for Boston, New England, on 4 June 1737, wrecked on Sable Island, Nova Scotia. [Pa Gaz. 6.9.1737]

CATHERINE, from Dublin *with 120 passengers* bound for Philadelphia, Pennsylvania, in 1741. [PaGaz.5 Nov 1741]

CATHERINE, master Thomas Leathes, from Cork bound for Nova Scotia, 1762. [APCCol.1762.467]

CATHERINE, Captain Bolton, from Cork bound for Jamaica, 1762. [APCCol.1762.467]

CATHERINE, Captain Fortune, from Cork to Maryland, 11 April 1774. [LL.533]

SHIPS FROM IRELAND TO EARLY AMERICA, 1623-1850, IV

CATHERINE, Captain Crawford, arrived in Boston during 1817 from Dublin. [LL.5183]

CATHERINE, arrived in Barbados on 16 November 1825 from Belfast. [LL.6079]

CERES OF DUBLIN, Captain Reed, from Dublin via Madeira to St Kitts, British West Indies, on 18 May 1764. [Dublin Journal: 19.5.1764]

CERES, Captain Hall, arrived in New York in June 1803 from Cork. [LL.4367]

CERES, Captain Quadrill, arrived in Philadelphia on 18 February 1819. [LL.5372]

CHARLES OF BRISTOL, arrived in Kinsale on 18 November 1667 from Barbados. [CSPIre.1667]

CHARLES, arrived in New York *with passengers* from Ireland on 29 May 1848; arrived in Baltimore, Maryland, on 1 February 1849 *with passengers* from Limerick. [IHR.39.156]

CHARLOTTE, 160 tons, Captain Curtis, from Waterford to Philadelphia, six voyages between 1766-1771. [W.399]

CHARLOTTE, master Robert Montgomery, from Newry *with passengers* bound for Philadelphia, Pennsylvania, arrived there on 14 June 1773.

CHARLOTTE, master Richard Curtis, from Waterford *with passengers* bound for Philadelphia, Pennsylvania, arrived there on 4 July 1773.

SHIPS FROM IRELAND TO EARLY AMERICA, 1623-1850, IV

CHARLOTTE, Captain Furlong, from Youghal *with passengers* bound for Newfoundland in May 1780. [FLJ.24-27 May 1780]; Captain Fisher, from Waterford to Grenada in 1792. [LL.2314]

CHARLOTTE, Captain Thom, arrived in Jamaica on 23 January 1827 from Cork. [LL.5163]

CHARLOTTE, Captain Laurence, from Belfast to Philadelphia, arrived in November 1818. [LL.5349]

CHARMING BETTY, master .... Driscoll, from Cork bound for St Kitts, British West Indies, in 1758, was captured by the French and taken to Guadeloupe, French West Indies, in 1758. [SM.21.50]

CHARMING MOLLY OF DUBLIN, returned to Dublin from Antigua, British West Indies, on 28 April 1741. [Dublin Newsletter: 28.4.1741]

CHARMING MOLLY, master ...... Martin, from Belfast bound for Jamaica, was captured by the French and taken to Guadeloupe, in 1756. [SM.18.626]

CHARMING MOLLY, master Anthony Roche, from Waterford bound for Louisbourg, New France, was captured by the French but ransomed for £800 in 1759. [SM.22.502]

CHARMING PEGGY, master .... Clark, from Dublin to Grenada in 1772. [LL.3741]

CHARMING POLLY, a brig, master George Mirren, from Londonderry to Baltimore, Maryland, in September 1773. [LJ:31.8.1773]

CHARMING SALLY, master ... Wallace, from Cork bound for Quebec, was captured by the French on 24 August 1760. [SM.22.502]

SHIPS FROM IRELAND TO EARLY AMERICA, 1623-1850, IV

CHATHAM, from Baltimore, Maryland, bound for Belfast, in 1771. [BNL.3.1771]

CHATHAM, arrived in Quebec on 18 August 1823 from Belfast. [LL.5839]

CHATSWORTH, Captain Nunna, from Cork to Dominica in 1775. [LL.669]

CHERRY, Vaptain Mayne, arrived in Newfoundland on 16 May 1826 from Waterford. [LL.6121]

CHERUB, Captain Hodgson, arrived in Barbados on 18 April 1826 from Dublin. [LL.6121]

CHICHESTER OF BELFAST, master Robert Lusk, from Belfast to York River, Virginia, 1745. [VaGaz]

CHILCOMBE, Captain Kavanagh, from Ross to Newfoundland in 1792. [LL.2315]

CHOTLEY, Captain Robinson, from Cork to Barbados, 15 December 1773. [LL.500]

CHRISTOPHER, arrived in New York on 12 September 1815 *with 50 passengers* from Belfast. [SM.77.952]

CHURCH OF BRISTOL, Captain Popplestone, arrived in Kinsale on 21 September 1668 from Barbados. [CSPIre.1668]

CITY OF CORK, from Cork to Barbados in 1825. [LL.6048]

CITY OF DERRY OF LONDONDERRY, a snow, from Newcastle, Delaware, bound for Ireland, 1747, 1749. [Davey and Carsan Letterbook in Library of Congress].

CLARE, master ..... Walsh, from Antigua bound for Dublin, was captured by the French and taken to Guadeloupe, French West Indies, in 1757. [SM.19.325]

CLARENCE, Captain Mundell, arrived in Halifax, Nova Scotia, on 9 January 1826 from Waterford. [LL.6091]

CLARENDON PACKET, Captain Amery, from Cork to Barbados, 26 December 1773. [LL.500]

CLIFTON, Captain Bryant, from Waterford to Newfoundland in 1775. [LL.664]

CLIMAX, Captain Merchant, from Dublin to Boston, Massachusetts, arrived on 5 Jun 1817 and in November 1818. [LL.5200/5349]

COHEN, Captain Davis, from Cork to Jamaica in 1790 and in 1792. [LL.2240/2316]

COLLINS, Captain Ashbridge, arrived in St Andrew's, New Brunswick, in June 1823 from Belfast. [LL.5823]

COLUMBIA, Captain Anderson, arrived in Trinidad on 13 February 1826 from Dublin. [LL.6106]

COLUMBUS, Captain Reid, from Cork to Jamaica in 1805. [LL.4227]

COLUMBUS, arrived in New York *with passengers* from Ireland on 9 May 1851. [IHR.39.156]

COMMERCE, from Limerick bound for Baltimore, Maryland, in 1772.

COMMERCE, Captain McDonald, arrived in St John, New Brunswick, on 11 June 1823 from Newry. [LL.5823]

COMMODORE, Captain Preble, arrived in New York on 16 December 1825 from Cork. [LL.6083]

CONNOLY, a brig, master Alexander Cain, from Dublin *with passengers* bound for Philadelphia, Pennsylvania, arrived there on 19 October 1772.

SHIPS FROM IRELAND TO EARLY AMERICA, 1623-1850, IV

CONNOLLY, a brig, from Dublin *with 65 passengers* bound for Philadelphia, Pennsylvania, in 1770. [Pa.Journal: 28 June 1770]; master Alexander Cain, from Dublin *with passengers* bound for Philadelphia, arrived there on 12 May 1772; master Alexander Cain, from Dublin *with passengers,* bound for Philadelphia, arrived there on 19 October 1772; from Dublin *with 65 passengers* bound for Philadelphia in 1773. [PaJournal: 27.10.1773]

CONSTANTINOPLE, Captain Ward, arrived in Kinsale in June 1667 bound for the West Indies. [CSPIre.1667]

CONSTITUTION, Captain Crosby, from Cork to Jamaica in 1825. [LL.6049]

CONTENT, master ..... Brown, from Waterford bound for Newfoundland, captured by Bayonne privateers in 1757. [SM.19.325]

CONYNGHAM, a brig, Captain Conyngham, from Londonderry *with 200 passengers* bound for Newcastle, Delaware, arrived in July 1789. [Pa. Packet: 11.8.1789]

CORNELIA, arrived in New York *with passengers* from Ireland on 4 September 1850. [IHR.39.156]

CORNWALLIS, Captain Anderson, from Cork on 9 November 1790 bound for Antigua. [LL.2244]

COUNTESS OF BUTE, arrived in Quebec on 29 June 1817 from Limerick. [LL.5201]

COUSINS, Captain Bliss, arrived in Newfoundland on 16 May 1826 from Waterford. [LL.6121]

CRAWFORD, master ..... Stokes, from Dublin bound for New York, captured by privateers from Cape Breton, Acadia, in 1756. [SM.18.626]

SHIPS FROM IRELAND TO EARLY AMERICA, 1623-1850, IV

CUMBERLAND, Captain Geraghty, from Dublin to Baltimore, Maryland, in 1825. [LL.6049]; Captain Geraghty, arrived in Baltimore on 23 May 1826 from Belfast. [LL.6130]

DALMARNOCK, arrived in Charleston, South Carolina, on 6 January 1826 from Cork. [LL.6089]

DAPHNE, Captain Banks, arrived in Newfoundland on 23 August 1823 from Waterford. [LL.5741]

DAVID, Captain Cannon, arrived in New York *with passengers* from Ireland on 30 September 1848. [IHR.39.156]

DAVID SHAW, Captain Harrison, arrived in Quebec on 3 July 1822 from Westport. [LL.5725]; Captain Harrison, arrived in St John, New Brunswick, in July 1823 from Belfast. [LL.5840]

DAWS, Captain Hunter, arrived in New York on 9 July 1817 from Belfast. [LL.5202]

DERWENT, Captain Harrison, arrived in St John, New Brunswick, on 13 June 1823 from Londonderry. [LL.5823]

DEVONSHIRE, Captain Fisher, from Cork to Antigua in 1775. [LL.666]

DIANA, Captain Ricas, arrived in New York on 1 May 1826 from Cork. [LL.6120]

DICKENSON, a snow, from Philadelphia, to Letterkenny, County Donegal, in February 1774. [PaGaz]

DILIGENT OF CORK, master John Cast, arrived in Kinsale in August 1669 from the Leeward Islands. [CSPIre.1669]

SHIPS FROM IRELAND TO EARLY AMERICA, 1623-1850, IV

DISPATCH OF BRISTOL, master Bonnell, from Cork bound for Halifax, Nova Scotia in 1759, was captured by the French. [SM.21.331]

DORSET, Captain Buck, arrived in Newfoundland in June 1823 from Waterford. [LL.5823]

DOVE, Captain Lecey, arrived in Newfoundland in June 1803 from Waterford. [LL.4367]

DREADNOUGHT, Captain Bread, from Waterford to Newfoundland, 13 April 1774. [LL.531]

DRITES, Captain Richardson, arrived in Halifax, Nova Scotia, in 1817 from Cork. [LL.5185]

DRUID, Captain Moore. From Dublin to St Vincent in 1805. [LL.4224]

DUBLIN, a vessel illegally trading between the ports of Dublin and Kinsale in Ireland and the American colonies, was seized by the Admiralty of England in 1679. [ActsPCCol.1679.1287]

DUBLIN MERCHANT, master Robert Ross, from Virginia to Dublin, in 1700. [TNA.CO5.1311.10.iii.400]

DUBLIN, master ... Tate, from New York bound for Dublin in 1759, was captured by the French but ransomed for £1500. [SM.21.217]

DUBLIN PACKET, from Dublin to New York in 1817, [LL.5184]; Captain Coles, from Dublin to New York, arrived on 30 November 1818. [LL.5348]; Captain McLean, arrived in New York on 10 February 1826 from Dublin. [LL.6103]; Captain Newcomb, arrived in New York on 22 May 1826 from Dublin. [LL.6121]

DUCHESS OF LEINSTER, 60 tons, Captain McCarthy, from Waterford to the West Indies, 1766-1771. [W.399]

DUKE OF BEDFORD, master .... Morison, from Londonderry bound for Antigua in 1758, was captured by the French and taken to Martinique, French West Indies. [SM.20.553]

DUKE OF YORK, 100 tons, Captain Weekes, from Waterford to Newfoundland in 1766-1771. [W.399]

DUMFRIES, Captain Hancock, arrived in Baltimore, Maryland, on 24 May 1826 from Belfast. [LL.6130]

DUNBAR, from Philadelphia, Pennsylvania, to Belfast in 1756. [PaGaz.]

DUNLOP, Captain Gowan, arrived in Charleston, South Carolina, on 18 February 1826 from Belfast, [LL.6104]; Captain Gowan, from Belfast *with passengers* bound for Baltimore, Maryland, in April 1829. [BNL:7.4.1829]

EAGLE, Captain Salmon, from Cork to Jamaica, 21 December 1773. [LL.500]

EAGLE, Captain Riches, arrived in New York in June 1803 from Belfast. [LL.4365]

EAGLE, Captain Thompson, from Londonderry to New York in 1805. [LL.4232]

EARL OF ABERDEEN, from Dublin to Miramachi, New Brunswick, in 1825. [LL.6056]; Captain Mears, arrived in Baltimore, Maryland, on 2 June 1826 from Belfast. [LL.6131]

EARL OF HOLDERNESS, from Belfast to Philadelphia, Pennsylvania, *with passengers* in 1752. [BNL]

SHIPS FROM IRELAND TO EARLY AMERICA, 1623-1850, IV

EARL FITZWILLIAM, Captain Storey, arrived in Dominica on 31 December 1816 from Cork. [LL.6164]

EARL TALBOT, arrived in Quebec in July 1822 from Cork. [LL.5726]

EASTER, Captain Brocklebank, from Cork to Halifax, Nova Scotia, in 1775. [LL.669]

EBENEZER Captain Hath, arrived in Newfoundland on 23 June 117 from Waterford. [LL.5197]

ECLIPSE, arrived in Quebec in July 1822 from Dublin. [LL.5726]

EDGELL, Captain Carroll, arrived in Newfoundland in June 1803 from Waterford. [LL.4366]

EDWARD, Captain Gray, arrived in Philadelphia on 23 December 1802 from Belfast. [LL.4323]

EDWARD AND ISAAC, from Cork bound for Jamaica, was captured by the French in 1759. [SM.21.271]

EDWARD DOWNES, arrived in the Mississippi on 2 February 1819 from Belfast, [LL.5372]; Captain Hussell, arrived in Halifax, Nova Scotia, in August 1822 from Belfast. [LL.724]; Captain Purdy, arrived in New Orleans on 30 January 1826 from Belfast. [LL.6105]

EIGHTY-THREE, Captain Scott, from Cork on 8 September 1783 bound for Antigua. [LL.1605]

ELCANO OF LIVERPOOL, Captain Joseph Whiteside, from Belfast bound for New York, was wrecked on the Hen and Chicken Rocks, Isle of Lewis, Outer Hebrides, on 11 December 1879.

ELIAS, Captain Ryan, arrived in Boston on 21 April 1719 from Belfast. [LL.5387]

ELINOR OF COLERAINE, from Portrush *with passengers* bound for America in 1754.

ELINOR, Captain Waters, from Cork to Barbados on 17 January 1772. [LL.3749]

ELIZA, Captain Wiseman, from Cork on 9 November 1790 bound for Dominica. [LL.2244]

ELIZA, Captain Muirhead, from Dublin to Jamaica in 1805. [LL.4230]

ELIZA, Captain Ryan, from Belfast to Boston, Massachusetts, in 1819. [LL.5387]

ELIZA ANN, Captain Malcolm, arrived in New York on 14 June 1818 from Limerick. [LL.5510]

ELIZA LIDDELL, from Sligo *with passengers,* landed at St John, New Brunswick, in July 1847.

ELIZABETH, from Dublin to Philadelphia, Pennsylvania, in 1729. [Dublin Gazette]

ELIZABETH, master William Browne, from Cork bound for Guadeloupe, French West Indies, in 1762. [APCCol.1762.467]; Captain Kennan, from Dublin to Jamaica in 1766. [LL.3175]

ELIZABETH, master Thomas Love, from Cork bound for Martinique, French West Indies, in 1762. [APCCol.1762.467]

ELIZABETH, Captain McLean, from Cork to Antigua in 1764. [LL.2966]

ELIZABETH, 55 tons, Captain Shanahan, from Waterford to Newfoundland in 1766-1771. [W.399]

ELIZABETH, Captain McNeil, from Cork on 29 June 1790 bound for Boston, New England. [LL.2245]

ELIZABETH, arrived in New York *with passengers* from Ireland on 16 May 1846. [IHR.39.156]

ELIZABETH AND CATHERINE OF NEW YORK, a snow, master John Lush, from New York bound for Belfast in December 1731, also in December 1732, returned to New York via the Isle of Maia; from New York bound for Belfast and returned to New York via Madeira in July 1734; arrived in New York in July 1735 from Belfast via the Isle of Maia. [TNA.CO5.114.111-112] [PRONI.D354.494]

ELIZABETH AND MARY, from Waterford bound for Jamaica, in 1762. [APCCol.1762.467]

ELIZABETH AND SARAH, from Dublin to Quebec in 1825, [LL.6055]; 330 tons, from Killala, County Mayo, July 1846, *with 276 passengers* bound for Quebec, landed there in September 1846.

ELLINOR OF WEYMOUTH, master Henry Guaden, from the Caribbees to Kinsale in 1638. [Harl.2048/311]

ELLIS OF CORK, master .... Gilsane, from Cork bound for Jamaica in 1758, was captured by the French. [SM.20.219]

ELWOOD, Captain Hodgson, from Cork on 10 September 1783 bound for Jamaica. [LL.1605]

ENDEAVOUR OF LIVERPOOL, master William Anyon, from Barbados to Belfast in 17... [PRONI.D354.440]

ENDEAVOUR, Captain Hearne, from New York bound for Belfast wrecked off the Outer Hebrides on 27 January 1790. [LL.2185]

EOLUS, arrived in Quebec in May 1826 from Waterford. [LL.6131]

ESME, Captain Thompson, from Londonderry to New York in 1805. [LL.4227]

ESSEX OF SALEM, from Dublin and Londonderry to New England in 1720. [Dublin Courant: 16.11.1719]

ESTHER, from Montserrat, British West Indies, to Belfast in 1755. [PRONI.D354.699]

ETHELRED, master Nicholas French, from Galway bound for Barbados in 1697, was captured by French privateers and taken to Martinique. [TNA.HCA.Exams.Vol.81.April,1698]

EWAN OF LIVERPOOL, Captain Taggart, from Londonderry *with passengers* bound for Quebec in May 1836. [LJ.10.5.1836]

EXCELSIOR, arrived in New York *with passengers* from Ireland on 27 September 1853. [IHR.39.156]

EXCHANGE, 100 tons, master Nicholas Burrows, from Bristol, England, via Cork bound for Nevis, British West Indies, in 1702. [APCCol.1702.860]

EXPERIMENT, Captain McConnell, from Dublin to Barbados on 14 January 1766. [LL.3133]

SHIPS FROM IRELAND TO EARLY AMERICA, 1623-1850, IV

EXPERIMENT, master John Downing, at Funchal, Madeira, 29 August 1791 when bound from Cork to Jamaica. [ARM.ms698]

FACTOR, Captain Cowan, arrived in New York on 24 June 1817 from Newry. [LL.5198]

FACTOR, Captain Prince, arrived in Baltimore, Maryland, on 25 April 1826 from Dublin. [LL.6119]

FAIR PLAY, Captain Griffin, arrived in New Orleans on 22 January 1819. [LL.5374]

FAITHFUL STEWARD, master Con. McCausland, from Londonderry *with 249 passengers* bound for Philadelphia, wrecked on the Capes of Delaware in September 1785. [Pennsylvania Packet 4.1.1786]

FAME, Captain Moore, from Dublin on 22 January 1772 bound for the West Indies. [LL.3749]

FAME PACKET, from Cork to Grenada in 1803. [LL.4340]

FAME, Captain Malcolm, from Belfast to Quebec in 1825. [LL.6048]

FAME, arrived in Jamaica from Cork in 1819, [LL.5385]; Captain Ocrat, arrived in Jamaica during February 1826 from Cork. [LL.6110]

FANNY, master Archibald Gardner, from Philadelphia to Ireland in 1754. [PRONI.D354.539]; from Newry bound for Philadelphia, Pennsylvania, in 1757, was captured by the French but later ransomed. [SM.19.325]

FANNY, arrived in Halifax, Nova Scotia, on 7 August 1823 from Cork. [LL.5837]

SHIPS FROM IRELAND TO EARLY AMERICA, 1623-1850, IV

FANNY, arrived in New York *with passengers* from Ireland on 1 May 1850. [IHR.39.156]

FAVOURITE, Captain Richardson, from Cork to Antigua in 1802. [LL.4319]

FIDELITY, Captain English, from Dublin to Quebec in 1825. [LL.6056]

FINGAL, arrived in New York *with passengers* from Ireland on 7 November 1848. [IHR.39.156]

FOGO, Captain Ash, from Waterford to Newfoundland in 1792. [LL.2318]

FOREST CHIEF, Captain A R Rettie, from New York bound for Londonderry, wrecked off Islay, Scotland, on 6 November 1872.

FORTESCUE, Captain Martin, from Dublin to Quebec in 1825. [LL.6055]; Captain Martin, arrived in Trinidad on 21 February 1826 from Dublin. [LL.6106]

FORTUNE OF DUBLIN, 90 tons, master Robert Holmes, from Ireland bound for Antigua in 1696 when captured by a French privateer and taken to Martinique. [TNA.HCA.Exams.Vol.81.April 1698]; a prize ship at Martinique, French West Indies, in 1698. [SPAWI.1698.660]

FORTUNE, Capyain Hunter, from Cork to Tortula on 6 September 1790. [LL.2238]

FOSTER, Captain Morse, arrived in New York on 4 July 1817 from Belfast. [LL.5202]

FOX, a snow, master James Drew, from Waterford via Madeira bound for Antigua, was attacked and captured by the French but liberated by the <u>Sturdy Beggar of New York</u>, a privateer, master Robert Troup, and landed in St John's, Antigua, during March 1760. [SM.22.220]

FRANCIS AND ELIZABETH, from Philadelphia, Pennsylvania, to Londonderry in 1742. [PaGaz]

FREDERICKTON, Captain Barnett, from Kinsale on 16 August 1823 bound for St John, New Brunswick. [LL.5840]

FREEMAN OF DUBLIN, arrived in Kinsale on 26 June 1668 from Virginia bound for Waterford. [CSPIre.1668]

FREEDOM OF WHITEHAVEN, from Dublin *with passengers* bound for America in 1730. [DWJ.28.2.1730]

FRIENDSHIP OF BELFAST, master John Collwell, from Virginia to Liverpool, England, in 1700. [TNA.CO5.1311/10.iii/400]; from Belfast to Charleston, South Carolina, 1718. [PRONI.354.369/370]

FRIENDSHIP, from Killibegs to Barbados in 1705. [PRONI.D501.1]

FRIENDSHIP OF BRISTOL, master ......Bogg, from Cork bound for the West Indies in 1758, was captured by the French. [SM.20.219]

FRIENDSHIP, a ship, from Bristol via Cork to St Kitts, British West Indies, in 1762. [NRS.CS96.4370]

FRIENDSHIP, Captain Roche, from Cork to Antigua on 14 January 1766. [LL.3127]

FRIENDSHIP, master William McCulloch, from Belfast *with passengers* bound for Philadelphia, Pennsylvania, arrived 15 October 1772.

FRIENDSHIP, master ....Greatruken, from Newfoundland to Youghal in 1772. [LL.3744]

FRIENDSHIP, Captain Ogilvie, from Cork to Jamaica, 21 December 1772. [LL.500]

FRODSHAM, a snow, master James Aspinal, from Londonderry *with passengers* bound for Philadelphia, Pennsylvania, arrived there in September 1735. [PaGaz]

GALE, from Baltimore, to Belfast, 1769. [BNL]

GALWAY PACKET, a brig, Captain Drummond, from Dublin via Teneriffe, Canary Islands, bound for New York in 1775. [TNA.AO12.30.306; 101.22; 109.192; AO13.65.155]

GANGES, Captain Mouat, arrived in New York on 16 April 1826 from Cork. [LL.6119]

GARRET, a sloop, from Dublin *with passengers* bound for New York 1730s

GARRICK, arrived in New York *with passengers* from Ireland on 25 May 1849. [IHR.39.156]

GENERAL ELLIOT, Captain Frank, arrived in Newfoundland on 12 July 1823 from Cork. [LL.5826]

GENERAL MONCKTON, Captain Tingley, from Cork bound for New York, 1762. [APCCol.1762.467]

GENERAL WASHINGTON, Captain Davis from Philadelphia to Dublin in 1793. [LL.2469]

GEORGE IV, Captain Murdoch, arrived in Barbados on 4 April 1826 from Cork. [LL.6124]

GEORGE, master Robert Crannel, from Dublin bound for Martinique, French West Indies, in 1762. [APCCol.1762.467]

GEORGE AND ELIZABETH, arrived in Quebec in July 1822 from Cork. [LL5726]

GEORGE AND MARY, from Cork to Quebec in 1825. [LL.6055]

GEORGE AND THOMAS, arrived in Barbados on 12 January 1826 from Dublin. [LL.6095]

GEORGE OF GLASGOW, from Dublin with 81 men and boys plus 26 women – all indentured servants – bound for Virginia in 1746. They mutinied when at sea and sailed the ship to Scotland where they were captured by the Royal Navy and presumably sent to America. [CM: June 1746]

GILBERT, Captain Henderson, arrived in Quebec in May 1826 from Dublin. [LL.6131]

GLENTANNER, Captain Sellar, arrived in St John, New Brunswick, on 23 July 1823 from Belfast. [LL.5840]

GLORIOUS MEMORY, Captain Wilson, from Cork to Quebec in 1766. [LL.3165]

GOLDEN LION OF BRISTOL, Captain Newer, arrived in Kinsale on 9 June 1668 bound for Virginia. [CSPIre.1668]

GOOD INTENT OF DUBLIN, 80 tons, was captured by the French and taken to St Malo, France, in 1756. [SM.18.626]

GOOD INTENT, 60 tons, Captain Pullen, from Waterford to Newfoundland in 1766-1771. [W.400]

GOOD KING, master .... Carlin, from Cork bound for Madeira, was captured by the French and taken to Martinique, French West Indies, in 1758. [SM.21.50]

GORRELL, master Thomas Rymer, from Cork bound for Jamaica, 1762. [APCCol.1762.467]

GRACE, master ..... Bible, from Cork bound for St Eustatia, Dutch West Indies, in 1756, was captured by the French and taken to Guadeloupe, French West Indies. [SM.19.164]

GRACE, master ..... French, from Dublin bound for Madeira and Antigua in 1759, captured by a privateer from Bayonne, France. [SM.21.157]

GRACE, a 140 ton brig, master Robert George, from Ireland *with passengers* bound for Baltimore, Maryland, in February 1784. [LJ: 6.1.1784]

GRACE AND MOLLY, from Belfast to New York in 1735 and 1736. [TNA.CO5.114]

GRAND DUKE OF YORK, arrived in Dublin on 17 August 1667 from Boston, New England. [CSPIre.1667]

GRAND TURK, from Belfast to New York in 1819. [LL.5387]

GRANDSON, master .... Maccarthie, from Cork bound for Madeira, captured by the French and taken to Martinique, French West Indies, in 1758. [SM.21.50]

GREENHOW, arrived in Quebec in May 1826 from Newry. [LL.6131]

GREYHOUND, master ..... Francis, from Waterford bound for Newfoundland, was captured by the <u>Aurora of Bayonne</u> a French privateer in 1760. [SM.22.334]

HAMILTON, master .... Parkinson, from Cork to Grenada in 1772. [LL.3740]

HAMILTON, Captain Williams, arrived in Quebec on 2 July 1823 from Belfast. [LL.5828]

HANNAH OF CORK, a brig, master Joseph Ruddock, from Jamaica to Bristol, England, in 1705. [TNA.SP63/365/127]

HANNAH, master .... Hoskins, from Cork, was captured by the French and taken to Martinique, French West Indies, in 1758. [SM.21.50]

HANNAH, master ..... Milliken, from Ireland bound for Jamaica, was captured by the French and taken to Martinique, French West Indies, in 1759. [SM.21.271]

HANNAH, master ....Green, from Dublin to St Eustatia, Dutch West Indies, in 1772. [LL.3742]

HANNAH, master James Mitchell, from Londonderry *with passengers* bound for Newcastle, Delaware, and Philadelphia, Pennsylvania, arrived 28 August 1772; master James Mitchell, from Londonderry *with passengers* bound for Newcastle, Delaware, and Philadelphia, Pennsylvania, arrived there on 8 August 1773; arrived in Londonderry from New York in March 1775. [BEP:4.3.1775]

HANNAH, Captain Graham, from Belfast to Quebec in 1825. [LL,6048]

HANNAH, Captain Cullen, from Dublin to Barbados in 1825. [LL.6048]; arrived in Barbados on 20 April 1826 from Dublin. [LL.6121]

HANOVER OF BELFAST, from Belfast to Charleston, South Carolina, in 1717. [PRONI.D354.363]

HAPPY RETURN, master ..... Stewart, from Philadelphia, Pennsylvania, bound for Londonderry, was captured by the French but later ransomed for £1000 in 1757. [SM.19.437]

HARMONY, Captain Gibson, arrived in Jamaica on 21 June 1817 from Belfast. [LL.5198]

HARMONY, arrived in New York *with passengers* from Ireland on 22 May 1851. [IHR.39.156]

HARRIET, Captain Carr, arrived in Quebec on 18 August 1823 from Belfast. [LL.5840]

HARRISON, Captain Wall, arrived in Quebec on 13 July 1823 from Londonderry. [LL.5830]

HATT, Captain Cuming, from Waterford to Newfoundland in 1805. [LL.4232]

HAVANNAH, a brig, Captain Sutter, from Newry *with 90 passengers* bound for Baltimore, arrived in July 1789. [Pennsylvania Packet: 31.7.1789]

HECTOR, master William Robinet, at Funchal, Madeira, 25 December 1792 when bound from Cork to Barbados. [ARM.699]

HELEN, a brig, Captain Fitzgerald, arrived in New York on 12 September 1815 *with 40 passengers* from Sligo. [SM.77.952]

HENRY, a galley, master Patrick Guin, at Funchal, Madeira, in October 1793 when bound from Cork to St Vincent, British West Indies. [ARM.ms699]

HENRY, Captain Coffin, from Cork to New York in 1803. [LL.4354]; Captain Penrice, arrived in Miramachi, New Brunswick, in July 1823 from Newry. [LL.5830]

HENRY GRINNELL, arrived in New York *with passengers* from Ireland on 16 August 1852. [IHR.39.156]

SHIPS FROM IRELAND TO EARLY AMERICA, 1623-1850, IV

HERO, from Cork to Antigua in 1805. [LL.4226]

HIBERNIA OF DUBLIN, from Dublin to Maryland in March 1740. [Dublin News-letter: 7.3.1740]

HIBERNIA, master .... Connor, from South Carolina bound for Lisbon, Portugal, in 1758, was captured by the French and taken to Cape Francois, St Dominique, French West Indies. [SM.21.158]

HIBERNIA, master ... Troy, bound from Philadelphia, Pennsylvania, to Dublin in 1759, was captured by the French but ransomed for £1000. [SM.21.272]

HIBERNIA, Captain Knethell, from Cork to Newfoundland in 1766. [LL.3167]

HIBERNIA, master William Keith, voyaging between Philadelphia, Pennsylvania, and Newcastle, Delaware, to Londonderry and return *with passengers* in the 1760s. [PaGaz: 15.11.1764; BNL: 26.7.1765; BNL: 16.6.1767]

HIBERNIA, Captain Wood, from Londonderry bound for Philadelphia, wrecked off Islay, Scotland, on 7 October 1808. [LL.4295]

HIBERNIA, Captain Fitzsimmons, arrived in Jamaica on 29 May 1817 from Belfast. [LL.6194]

HIBERNIA, arrived in Quebec in July 1822 from Waterford. [LL.5726]

HIBERNIA, Captain Green, from Cape Breton to Cork in 1825. [LL.5974]

HIBERNIA, Captain Walteling, arrived in New York on 25 June 1823 from Dublin, [LL.5825]; Captain Raynee, arrived in Barbados on 27 April 1826 from Cork. [LL.6124]

HIGHLANDER, Captain Gardner, from Londonderry *with passengers* bound for St John, New Brunswick, in May 1836. [LJ.10.5.1836]

HINDLEY, Captain Cowell, from Cork to St Vincent in 1774. [LL.549]

HIPPOCAMPI, Captain Tessler, arrived in Newfoundland on 2 July 1823 from Belfast. [LL.5284]

HOLLAND, Captain Taylor, from Cork to Jamaica, 13 December 1773. [LL.500]

HONOUR AND MOLLY, master .... Keating, from Waterford bound for New York, was captured by the French in 1759. [SM.21.331]

HOPE OF DUBLIN, 150 tons, arrived in Galway in August 1667 from Barbados; arrived in Dublin on 8 October 1667. [CSPIre.1667]

HOPE, Captain Smith, from Cork to Newfoundland in 1766. [LL.3167]

HOPE, Captain Jefford, from Dublin to Barbados in 1766. [LL.3166]

HOPE, Captain Harvey, from Cork to Newfoundland on 6 September 1790. [LL.2238]

HOPE, arrived in Quebec on 2 July 1822 from Dublin. [LL.5726]

HOPE KIRK, Captain Campbell, from Cork to Jamaica in 1766. [LL.3167]

HOPEWELL OF BRISTOL, 200 tons, from Antigua via Nevis, British West Indies, in July 1671 bound for England, 'unseaworthy', landed at Kinsale later in Cork. [Acts PCCol.1672.950]

HOPEWELL OF GALWAY, from Galway to Barbados 1660s. [ActsPCCol.1668.744]

HOPEWELL OF KINGSALE, from Kinsale to Maryland, 1664. [ActsPCCol.1668.765]

HOPEWELL OF DUBLIN, master James White, from Virginia to Buensores [Spain?] 1700. [TNA.CO5.1311.10.iii.400]

HOPEWELL, from Belfast *with passengers* bound for South Carolina via Philadelphia, in 1729. [PaGaz]

HOPEWELL, master Andrew Faucet, from Londonderry *with passengers* bound for Philadelphia, Pennsylvania, arrived there in September 1735. [PaGaz]

HOPEWELL, master Richard Twine, from Bristol and Cork bound for Jamaica, in 1762. [APCCol.1762.467]

HOPEWELL, master John Winning, from Londonderry *with passengers* bound for Philadelphia, Pennsylvania, arrived on 21 October 1772.

HORIZON, Captain Clark, arrived in New York on 7 August 1823 from Cork. [LL.836]

HOW, master .... Elbeck, from Belfast bound for Guadeloupe and Jamaica, captured by the French and taken to Martinique. French West Indies, in 1759. [SM.21.605]

HOWARD, Captain Stocking, arrived in New York on 24 July 1823 from Cork. [LL.5830]

HUGH, Captain McCracken, from Dublin to Quebec in 1825. [LL.6050]

HUGH AND JAMES, Captain McCarty, from Dublin to Philadelphia in 1766. [LL.3166]

HUNTINGTON, arrived in Baltimore, Maryland, *with passengers* from Limerick, Ireland, on 24 January 1849. [IHR.39.156]

HYNDMAN, a brig, Captain Follius, from Dublin and Cork to Barbados and Antigua in January 1816. [SNK:9.1.1816]

INDUSTRY, master ..... Galloway, from Cork bound for St Eustatia, Dutch West Indies, was captured by the French and taken to Martinique in 1757. [SM.19.325]

INDUSTRY, master William Moreton, from Cork bound for Guadeloupe, French West Indies, in 1762. [APCCol.1762.467]

INDUSTRY, from Dublin *with 24 passengers* bound for Philadelphia, Pennsylvania, in 1768.

INDUSTRY, 60 tons, Captain Doyle, from Waterford to Newfoundland between 1766 and 1771. [W.400]

INDUSTRY, Captain Morrison, arrived in Trinidad in 1819 from Belfast. [LL.5383]

INTREPID, Captain Bryce, from Londonderry *with passengers* bound for St John, New Brunswick, in May 1836. [LJ.10.5.1836]

SHIPS FROM IRELAND TO EARLY AMERICA, 1623-1850, IV

IRIS, Captain Smith, arrived in New York on 31 June 1818 from Dublin. [LL.5510]

IRISH OAK, master .... Semple, from Newry bound for Antigua in 1760, captured by the French. [SM.23.165]

IRISH VOLUNTEER, Captain Hodret, from Cork to Halifax, Nova Scotia, on 6 September 1790. [LL.2238]

ISAAC OF PROVIDENCE, arrived in Westport, Ireland, on 7 June 1696. [APCCol.VI.vii]

ISAAC OF BELFAST, from Charleston, South Carolina, to Belfast, in 1734. [PRONI.D354.491]

ISAAC, Captain Cragg, from Cork 1 February 1772 bound for Dominica. [LL.3752]

ISABELLA, Captain Booth, from Dublin to Quebec in 1825. [LL.6048]

JAMES OF BELFAST, master Henry Wilkinson, from Belfast to Antigua and Nevis in 1665, impressed into government service there, captured by the French off Guadeloupe, French West Indies, in the 1660s. [ActsPCCol.1668.755][PRONI.MIC19/1]

JAMES OF LONDON, master John Ashley, from Cork to Nevis, British West Indies, in 1679. [LRS.36.127]

JAMES, from Dublin *with passengers* bound for Newcastle, Delaware, in April 1728. [Memoirs of an Unfortunate Young Nobleman, James Annesley, 1743, BL.243.I.4]

JAMES, Captain Dixon, from Cork to St Vincent in 1802. [LL.4322]

SHIPS FROM IRELAND TO EARLY AMERICA, 1623-1850, IV

JAMES, Captain Sheats, arrived in Trinidad in February 1819 from Belfast. [LL.5373]

JAMES, arrived in Quebec in July 1822 from Newry. [LL.5726]

JAMES, Captain Johnson, arrived in Quebec on 9 July 1822 from Sligo. [LL.5728]

JAMES BAILLIE, from Belfast, arrived in Halifax, Nova Scotia, on 24 May 1817 bound for Quebec. [LL.6192]

JANE, master Robert Murray, from Belfast bound for Virginia in 1691, but was captured by a French privateer off Newfoundland in 1692 on homeward voyage. [TNA.HCA.Exams.Vol.80.January 1693]

JANE, master .... Sloane, from Cork bound for Antigua in 1758, captured by the French but ransomed for 440 guineas. [SM.20.331]

JANE, Captain Murdoch, arrived in Quebec on 28 June 1817 from Cork. [LL.5195]

JANE, arrived in Quebec in July 1822 from Waterford. [LL.5726]

JANE E. WALSH, arrived in New York *with passengers* from Ireland on 21 June 1846. [IHR.39.156]

JANE, Captain Johnson, from Sligo to Quebec in 1825. [LL.6055]

JANET, arrived in Quebec on 31 July 1823 from Ross. [LL.5836]

JANUS, Captain Beveridge, arrived in Quebec on 27 June 1817 from Limerick. [LL.5201]

SHIPS FROM IRELAND TO EARLY AMERICA, 1623-1850, IV

JEANE OF DUBLIN, master William Thornton, from Virginia to Buensores [Spain?] 1700. [TNA.CO5.1311.10.iii.400]

JEANNIE, master James Kirkwood, from Cork to America in 1775. [CBC]

JEANY, arrived in Newfoundland in June 1803 from Ross. [LL.4367]

JENNIFER, from Baltimore, Maryland, to Belfast in 1769. [BNL]

JENNY, from Londonderry *with passengers* bound for Newcastle, Delaware, in 1730, landed in Virginia. [PaGaz: 10.2.1730]

JENNY, master ..... Collison, from Cork to Montserrat in 1772. [LL.3742]

JENNY, master James Campbell, from Cork *with passengers* bound for Philadelphia, Pennsylvania, arrived 16 October 1772; masters James Campbell or Alexander McIlraith, from Londonderry *with passengers* bound for Newcastle, Delaware, and Philadelphia, Pennsylvania, arrived there on 25 June 1773.

JENNY, Captain Stewart, from Barbados bound for Londonderry, wrecked in the Sound of Isla, Mull, Scotland, on 25 January 1794. [LL.2586]

JESSIE, Captain Winslow, from Cork to South Carolina 14 January 1766. [LL.3127]

JESSY, Captain Hardy, from Cork to Dominica in 1805. [LL.4224]

JOHANNA, 120 tons, master Richard Burbridge, via Ireland bound for Virginia, 1702. [APCCol.1702.860]

SHIPS FROM IRELAND TO EARLY AMERICA, 1623-1850, IV

JOHN OF LONDON, master William Mabbett, when bound from Barbados to Galway, Limerick or Tralee, was captured by a Parliamentary ship in 1646. [TNA.HCA13.61/62]

JOHN OF DUBLIN, master John Videll, arrived in Virginia with passengers by 1724. [WI.22/23]

JOHN, Captain Wallace, from Cork to Grenada, 13 December 1773. [LL.500]

JOHN, Captain Cuthbert, from Cork to Antigua in 1775. [LL.669]

JOHN, arrived in Jamaica from Cork in 1819. [LL.5385]

JOHN, Captain Dickenson, arrived in New York on 18 April 1826 from Belfast. [LL.6119]

JOHN AND CHRISTIAN OF BRISTOL, [350 tons], at Kinsale on 21 January 1668 when bound for Virginia. [CSPIre.1668]

JOHN AND DAVID OF GLASGOW, arrived in Philadelphia, Pennsylvania, from Belfast, in 1729, also in June 1730. [PaGaz]

JOHN AND EDWARD, Captain Giles, from Liverpool and Belfast to New York, arrived on 1 December 1818. [LL.5348]; Captain King, arrived in Philadelphia on 14 July 1823 from Londonderry. [LL.5828]

JOHN AND ELIZABETH, Captain Cornish, from Cork to Dominica in 1766. [LL.3167]

JOHN AND FRANCES, Captain Helwell, arrived in Kinsale on 27 April 1669 from Virginia bound for Chester. [CSPIre.1669]

SHIPS FROM IRELAND TO EARLY AMERICA, 1623-1850, IV

JOHN AND LUCY, arrived in New York *with passengers* from Ireland on 20 May 1853. [IHR.39.156]

JOHN AND MARGARET, master Archibald McSparran, from Belfast *with passengers* bound for Newcastle, Delaware, and Philadelphia, Pennsylvania, in 1735. [LCCH.Wills.a1/23]

JOHN AND MATTY, Captain Russell, from Cork to Antigua in 1774. [LL.551]

JOHN AND SUSAN, from Waterford bound for Newfoundland in 1798. [PROI.Lecky pp]

JOHN BRIGHT, arrived in New York *with passengers* from Ireland on 21 April 1854, also on 28 August 1854. [IHR.39.156]

JOHN FULDEN, arrived in New York *with passengers* from Ireland on 18 August 1849. [IHR.39.156]

JOHN HOWARD, Captain Bruce, arrived in Quebec in May 1826 from Cork. [LL.6131]

JOHN MCCANNON, Captain Larimar, arrived in Charleston, South Carolina, on 18 February 1817 from Cork. [LL.6164]

JOSEPH OF BRISTOL, Captain William Jones, arrived in Kinsale in April 1669 from Virginia. [CSPIre.1669]

JOSEPH AND JANE, Captain Baird, from Belfast to Quebec in 1825. [LL.6049]

JOSEPHA, Captain French, from Cork bound for Jamaica, 1762. [APCCol.1762.467]

JOSEPH GREEN, Captain Lipscomb, arrived in Barbados on 28 February 1826 from Kinsale. [LL.6107]

SHIPS FROM IRELAND TO EARLY AMERICA, 1623-1850, IV

JOSEPH HOME, arrived in St John, New Brunswick, in April 1826 from Cork. [LL]

JOSHUA, Captain Hamilton, from Cork on 9 November 1790 bound for Dominica. [LL.2244]

JULIE OF MEMEL, Captain Holmann, from Belfast to Philadelphia, wrecked off the Outer Hebrides on 16 September 1878.

JUNE, Captain Merrylaw, arrived in New York in June 1803 from Galway. [LL.4367]

JUPITER, master John Perkins, from Cork bound for Jamaica and Havanna, Cuba, in 1762. [APCCol.1762.467]

JUPITER, master Michael Connor, from Liverpool and Cork bound for Barbados, 1762. [APCCol.1762.467]

JUPITER, Captain Gould, from Cork bound for Jamaica, 1762. [APCCol.1762.467]

JUPITER, master ….. Morris, from St Kitts to Dublin in 1772. [LL.3742]

JUPITER, master Alexander Ewing, from Londonderry *with passengers* bound for Newcastle, Delaware, and Philadelphia, Pennsylvania, arrived 16 June 1772; master Alexander Ewing, from Newry *with passengers* bound for Newcastle, Delaware, and Philadelphia, Pennsylvania, arrived 1 May 1773; master John Ewing, from Londonderry *with passengers* bound for Newcastle, Delaware, and Philadelphia, Pennsylvania, arrived 3 August 1773; Captain Ewing, arrived in Londonderry from New York in March 1775. [BEP: 4.3.1775]

KANGAROO, from Cork *with passengers* bound for New York in 1860. [PRONI.T3234.102]

SHIPS FROM IRELAND TO EARLY AMERICA, 1623-1850, IV

KATHERINE OF LONDONDERRY, master .... Cruikshanks, arrived in Virginia *with passengers* by 1692. [WI.28]

KELTON, Captain Brocklebank, from Dublin to Quebec in 1825. [LL.6049]]

KENT OF BIDDEFORD, master ..... Brady, from Waterford bound for New England in 1759, captured by the French and taken to Vigo, Spain. [SM.21.331]

KENT, arrived in Quebec in July 1822 from Londonderry. [LL.5726]

KING GEORGE, 100 tons, from Waterford to Newfoundland, six times between 1766 and 1771. [W.400]

KING OF PRUSSIA, master .... MacNamary, from New York bound for Belfast, captured by the French and taken to Vigo, Spain, in 1760. [SM.22.271]

KITTY, master John French, from Bristol and Cork bound for Antigua, British West Indies, in 1762. [APCCol.1762.467]

KITTY, a brigantine, master William Gordon, from Waterford bound for New York, 1762. [APCCol.1762.467]

KITTY, Captain Butler, from Cork to Newfoundland in 1764. [LL.2966]

KITTY, Captain Redmayne, from Cork to St Kitts in 1802. [LL.4315]

KOULI KHAN, from Ireland *with passengers* bound for Philadelphia, Pennsylvania, in 1744. [PaGaz]

LABRADOR PACKET, Captain Flynn, from Youghal *with passengers* bound for Newfoundland in May 1780. [FLJ.24-27 May 1780]

LACKY, Captain Brown, from Cork to Philadelphia in 1766. [LL.3168]

LADY ELIZABETH, Captain Wemyss, from Cork to Jamaica in 1766. [LL.3172]

LADY JANE, Captain Coaksley, from Dublin to Antigua in 1803. [LL.4344]

LADY KENMORE, Captain Smith, from Cork to Jamaica in 1803. [LL.4329]

LAMB OF DUBLIN, master William Burnside, from Liverpool *with passengers* bound for Virginia in 1698, [LRO]; master Richard Murfey, from Virginia to Dublin, 1700. [TNA.CO5.1311.10.iii.400]

LAMB, from New York bound for Dublin in December 1732, and return. [TNA.CO5.114.111]

LARCH, from Sligo *with 440 passengers* bound for Canada 1847

LARK, a brigantine, master ..... Cableman, from Cork, captured by the French and taken to Martinique, French West Indies, in 1759. [SM.21.557]

LARK, a schooner, from Newburyport, Massachusetts, to Newry in 1772.

LAUREL, 130 tons, from Belfast to Virginia in 1703. [TNA.CO5.1441]; from Belfast {?} to Virginia and Newfoundland in 1705. [PRONI.D501.1]

LAVINIA, Captain Brown, arrived in Halifax, Nova Scotia, on 23 May 1817 from Cork. [LL.6192]; Captain May, arrived in Quebec on 9 July 1822 from Dublin. [LL.5728]

LAVINIA, Captain Digby, arrived in Trinidad on 27 February 1826 from Belfast. [LL.6106]

LAWSON, a brigantine, master Benjamin Lowes, from Londonderry *with passengers* bound for Philadelphia, Pennsylvania, arrived there in September 1735. [PaGaz]

LAWSON, master ..... Chamberlain, from Dublin bound for Virginia in 1757, captured by the French but ransomed for 550 guineas. [SM.21.109]

L'BLOND, master William McNamara, from Cork bound for Jamaica and Havanna, Cuba, in 1762. [APCCol.1762.467]

LEIBOVITZ, arrived in New York *with passengers* from Ireland on 4 January 1854. [IHR.39.156]

LIBERTY, Captain Thompson, from Cork to Halifax, Nova Scotia, in 1790. [LL.2233]

LIBERTY AND PROPERTY, master .... Edgar, from Belfast bound for Barbados in 1758, captured by the French and taken to Guadeloupe, French West Indies. [SM.20.275]

LIDDELL, Captain Wheatley, arrived in Quebec on 14 August 1823 from Belfast. [LL.5839]

LINENHALL, Captain O'Neill, from Dublin to Jamaica in 1792. [LL.2318]

LION OF DUBLIN, from Barbados to Virginia in 1698. [TNA.HCA.Exams.Vol.81.April, 1700]

SHIPS FROM IRELAND TO EARLY AMERICA, 1623-1850, IV

LITTLE BEN, Captain Rosayne, from Youghal to Newfoundland in 1792. [LL.2313]

LITTLE JOHN, from Cork bound for Jamaica in 1758, also in1759, captured by the French and taken to Port au Prince, Haiti, French West Indies. [SM.20.389; 21.109]

LIVERPOOL, arrived in New York *with passengers* from Ireland on 18 June 1846. [IHR.39.156]

LLOYDS, from Cork to Quebec in 1825. [LL.6055]

LOGAN, Captain Kerr, arrived in Jamaica on 18 November 1825. [LL.6081]

LONDON, Captain Brown, arrived in Philadelphia on 20 July 1822 from Londonderry. [LL.5727]

LONDON PACKET, Captain Aspell, arrived in Newfoundland in July 1822 from Coleraine. [LL.5727]

LORD ASHBURTON, with 477 passengers, landed at Quebec, on 30 October 1847

LORD FREDERICK, Captain McLean, from Cork on 19 June 1764 bound for Grenada. [LL.2973]

LORD SYDENHAM, from Limerick *with 700 passengers* bound for Quebec, 1846.

LORD WELLINGTON, arrived in Quebec in July 1822 from Newry. [LL.5726]

LOUISA, master James Moore, at Funchal, Madeira, 11 October 1793 when bound from Cork to St Kitts, British West Indies. [ARM.ms699]

LOUISE, Captain Reeves, arrived in New York on 13 March 1826 from Belfast. [LL.6109]

SHIPS FROM IRELAND TO EARLY AMERICA, 1623-1850, IV

LOVELY BIDDY, from Waterford to Newfoundland, between 1766 and 1771. [W.401]

LOVEY JANE, master ..... Foster, from Belfast bound for Jamaica, captured by the French in 1757. [SM.19.613]

LOVELY JANE, master ....Hill, from Dublin to Antigua in 1772. [LL.3742]

LOVELY JEAN OF CORK, from Cork to St Kitts and St Eustatia, Dutch West Indies, in 1772. [NRS.AC20.2.29]

LOVELY PEGGY, 90 tons, Captain Weekes, from Waterford to the West Indies, 1766-1771. [W401]

LOWSON, master James Kirkpatrick, from Londonderry w*ith passengers* bound for Newcastle, Delaware, and Philadelphia, Pennsylvania, arrived there 8 September 1773.

LOYAL MERCHANT, master Thomas Langhorne, from Bristol, England, via Cork bound for Maryland, 1720. [TNA.E190.1187/1]

LOYALTY, from Belfast to Virginia in 1701. [TNA.CO5.1441]

LOVELY MELORA, master .....Hogan, from Limerick bound for Barbados, captured by the French and taken to Guadeloupe or Martinique, French West Indies, in 1757. [SM.19.493][LL.4337]

LUCANIA, arrived in New York *with passengers* from Ireland on 26 September 1851. [IHR.39.156]

LUCY, Captain Lamont, from Charleston, South Carolina, bound for Belfast, was wrecked in the Solway Firth, Dumfries-shire, Scotland, on 19 March 1803. [

SHIPS FROM IRELAND TO EARLY AMERICA, 1623-1850, IV

LUCY, Captain Fell, arrived in Halifax, Nova Scotia, on 30 April 1817 from Cork. [LL.5185]

LYDIA AND JANE, master Francis Brison, from Cork bound for Martinique, French West Indies, in 1762. [APCCol.1762.467]

LYON OF LIVERPOOL, 44 tons, master John Compton, from Liverpool via Cork and Waterford to Nevis and Montserrat, British West Indies, in 1681, and return to Chester, England. [LRS.36.196]

MACEDONIA, arrived in New York *with passengers* from Ireland on 7 May 1846. [IHR, 39.156]

MARATHON, Captain Crosby, arrived in Jamaica on 1 June 1817 from Belfast. [LL.6194]

MARATHON, arrived in New York *with passengers* from Ireland on 9 March 1853. [IHR.39.156]

MARCUS, Captain Hill, from Londonderry to St John, New Brunswick, in 1825. [LL.6056]

MARGARET, Captain Hearn, arrived in Quebec on 13 August 1823 from Ross. [LL.5840]

MARGARET, Captain Paterson, arrived in Jamaica in February 1826 from Belfast. [LL.6107]

MARGARETHA, Captain Tabetha, arrived in Charleston, South Carolina, on 5 January 1803 from Cork. [LL.4340]

MARIA, an American schooner, master John Eldridge, at Funchal, Madeira, on 17 June 1791 when bound from Dublin to the West Indies. [ARM.ms698]

MARS, Captain Hunter, arrived in Philadelphia in June 1803 from Dublin. [LL.4366]

MARQUIS OF ROCKINGHAM, Captain Barrow, from Cork to Jamaica in 1772. [LL.3742]

MARTHA, master ...... Rimmer, from Cork to Jamaica in 1772. [LL.3744]

MARTHA AND ANNE, master ...... Collings, from Waterford bound for Newfoundland, captured by Bayonne privateers from France in 1757. [SM.19.325]

MARTHA AND ELIZABETH, from Londonderry *with 170 passengers* bound for Philadelphia, Pennsylvania, landed in New York, 1728. [DI.15.2.1729]

MARY, master ..... Andrews, from Waterford bound for Newfoundland, captured by the French in 1757. [SM.19.437]

MARY, master .... Moon, from Cork bound for Guadeloupe, was captured by the French and taken to Martinique, French West Indies, in 1760. [SM.22.669]

MARY, a brig, master Edward Fearson, from St Kitts, British West Indies, to Cork, 1760. [NRS.CS96.4370]

MARY OF CORK, master William Dowly, arrived in Charleston, South Carolina, in 1763. [TNA.CO5.510]

MARY, Captain Tubb, from Cork to Newfoundland in 1766. [LL.3171]

MARY, 50 tons, Captain Hurley, from Waterford to Newfoundland in 1766-1771. [W.401]

SHIPS FROM IRELAND TO EARLY AMERICA, 1623-1850, IV

MARY, master Stephen Forrestal, from Waterford *with passengers* bound for Newfoundland in 1767

MARY, Captain Warden, from St Kitts bound for Londonderry, wrecked on the Mull of Kintyre, Argyll, Scotland, on 18 August 1767. [LL.3295]

MARY, 60 tons, Captain O'Brian, from Waterford to Newfoundland, 1769-1771. [W401]

MARY, Captain Tubman, from Cork on 12 September 1784 bound for Jamaica. [LL.1605]

MARY, Captain Ellis, arrived in Tortula on 16 September 1784 from Cork. [LL.1606]

MARY, a brig, Captain Cassidy, from Londonderry *with passengers* bound for Newcastle and Philadelphia, landed in December 1789. [Pennsylvania Packet: 5.12.1789]

MARY, from Belfast bound for Jamaica on 28 September 1790. [LL.2237]

MARY, Captain Neil, from Cork on 13 October 1790 bound for New York. [LL.2240]

MARY, Captain Jamieson, arrived in Jamaica on 19 November 1802 from Cork. [LL.4319]

MARY, Captain Southwick, from Belfast to New York in 1805. [LL.4232]

MARY, an American ship, master 'Abeather' Clark, at Funchal, Madeira on 5 March 1808 when bound from Belfast to Charleston, South Carolina. [ARM.CM696]; Captain Clark, arrived in Quebec on 2 July 1823 from Belfast. [LL.5828]

SHIPS FROM IRELAND TO EARLY AMERICA, 1623-1850, IV

MARY, Captain Yeoward, arrived in Quebec on 13 August 1823 from Dublin. [LL.5840]

MARY, Captain Wilson, from Dublin to Quebec in 1825. [LL.6049]; Captain Duncan, arrived in Quebec in May 1826 from Dublin. [LL.6131]

MARY, Captain Ainsley, from Londonderry to Quebec in 1825. [LL.6050]

MARY, Captain Wyman, from Cork *with passengers* bound for Boston, Massachusetts, arrived 17 May 1847, landed in Halifax, Nova Scotia. [Boston Liberator]

MARY ANNE, master .... Driscoll, from Cork bound for St Kitts, British West Indies, captured by the French and taken to Martinique, in 1759. [SM.22.105]

MARY ANN, Captain Frayne, from Dublin to the West Indies, 28 December 1773. [LL.500]

MARY AND BARBARA, Captain Riorden, from Cork to Baltimore, Maryland, in 1764. [LL.2976]

MARY AND BELL, bound from Ireland to Quebec in 1817. [PROI.CE.bundle 1a-3a-2, number 50]

MARY AND JANE, from Belfast to Boston in 1819. [LL.5387]

MARY AND JOE, arrived in Boston on 21 April 1819 from Belfast. [LL.5387]

MARY ANN, arrived in Quebec on 3 July 1822 from Limerick. [LL.5725]

MARY PEATON, Captain Caton, from Cork to Jamaica, 12 April 1774. [LL.531]

MAURICE AND MALLY, master ....Jago, from Newfoundland to Waterford in 1772. [LL.3741]; 70 tons, from Waterford to Newfoundland, 1766-1771. [W.401]

MAY, 180 tons, Captain Neville, from Waterford to Newfoundland between 1766 and 1771. [W401]

MAY, Captain Pollock, arrived in Antigua on 18 April 1826 from Belfast. [LL.6121]

MAYFLOWER, arrived in Halifax, Nova Scotia, in November 1818 from Dublin. [LL.5350]

MAYFLOWER, arrived in New York *with passengers* from Ireland on 7 October 1854. [IHR.39.156]

MECHANIC'S OWN, arrived in New York *with passengers* from Ireland on 15 September 1851. [IHR.39.156]

MENTOR, master Evan Evanson, from Cork bound for Jamaica, 1762.

MERCURY, Captain Ashmead, from Cork on 10 June 1764 bound for Philadelphia. [LL.2976]

MERCURY, Captain Mally, from Dublin to Antigua in 1766. [LL.3166]

MERCURY, Captain Kelick, from Cork bound for Barbados, was captured by a French privateer off Cape Clear, Ireland, in 1793. [SM.55.306]

MESSINA, master ..... Power, from Cork bound for St Eustatia, Dutch West Indies, in 1756, captured by the French. [SM.19.53]

METEOR, Captain Huttleston, arrived in New York on 22 May 1826 from Belfast. [LL.6121]

SHIPS FROM IRELAND TO EARLY AMERICA, 1623-1850, IV

MILFORD, Captain Shaw, via Cork to Jamaica in 1784. [BJ:27.11.1784]

MINERVA, master .... Farwell, from Cork bound for Newfoundland in 1758, captured by the French. [SM.20.331]

MINERVA, Captain Pocock, from Cork to Dominica, 13 December 1773. [LL.500]

MINERVA, master Francis Faires, from Newry *with passengers* bound for Philadelphia, Pennsylvania, arrived there on 11 June 1773.

MINERVA, Captain Neil, from Belfast bound for Jamaica, captured by the French and taken to L'Orient, France, in 1792. [SM.55.150]

MINERVA, Captain Pinkham, from Dublin *with passengers* bound for Charleston, South Carolina, in 1800. [Freeman's Journal: 4.9.1800]

MINERVA, arrived in Halifax, Nova Scotia, on 3 July 1817 from Cork. [LL.5201]

MOLLY, master ..... Brocking, from Cork bound for Newfoundland, captured by the French but later ransomed for 25,000 livres in 1757. [SM.19.325]

MOLLY, master John Smith, from Cork bound for the Leeward Islands, British West Indies, in 1762. [APCCol.1762.467]

MOLLY, 70 tons, Captain Keene, from Waterford to Newfoundland, 1766-1771. [W401]

MONARCH, from Cork to Quebec in 1825. [LL.6055]

MONTAGUE, Captain Edgar, arrived in Jamaica in May 1826 from Cork. [LL.6129]

MORNING STAR, master ... Welch, from Philadelphia, Pennsylvania, bound for Cork, captured by the French but ransomed in 1758. [SM.20.498]

MORO CASTLE, Captain Scott, from Cork bound for Jamaica, 1762. [APCCol.1762.467]

MORRISTOWN, Captain Dunbar, arrived in St John, New Brunswick, on 11 June 1823 from Kinsale. [LL.5823]

MORTIMER LIVINGSTON, arrived in New York *with passengers* from Ireland on 6 September 1851. [IHR.39.156]

MOUNT VERNON, arrived in Philadelphia on 5 May 1826 from Ireland. [LL.6122]

MOZAMBIQUE, from Sligo *with passengers* bound for New York in 1849. [Ballina Chronicle: 16.5.1849]

MULBERRY, master Turnover, from Philadelphia, Pennsylvania, to Kinsale in 1740. [LL.562]

MYRTILLA, from Cork *with 37 passengers* bound for Philadelphia, Pennsylvania, in the 1770s.

NANCY, master ..... Welch, from Ireland, captured by the French and taken to Guadeloupe, French West Indies, in 1758. [SM.20.498]

NANCY, master ..... Mackie, from Londonderry bound for Antigua, captured by the French and taken to Guadeloupe, French West Indies, in 1758. [SM.20.498]

NANCY, master .... Lathwaite, from Liverpool via Cork bound for Tortula, British West Indies, captured by the

SHIPS FROM IRELAND TO EARLY AMERICA, 1623-1850, IV

French and taken to Martinique, French West Indies, in 1760. [SM.22.386]

NANCY, a sloop, master Edward Manlove, from Bristol, England, and Cork bound for Martinique, French West Indies, in 1762. [APCCol.1762.467]

NANCY, master Joseph Mulls, from Liverpool and Cork bound for Jamaica, 1762. [APCCol.1762.467]

NANCY, Captain Chisholm from Cork to Jamaica on 11 January 1766, [LL.3131]; Captain Bell, from Cork to Antigua in 1772. [LL.3744]; Captain Jackson, from Cork to Dominica, 13 April 1774. [LL.531]

NANCY, Captain Payne, from Waterford to Newfoundland in 1774. [LL.551]

NANCY, Captain Ledgard, from Waterford to Newfoundland in 1774. [LL.551]

NANCY OF LONDONDERRY, Captain Thomas Crawford, from Londonderry *with 300 passengers* bound for Newcastle, Delaware, arrived there on 2 September 1789. [Pennsylvania Packet: 4.9.1789]

NAUTILUS, arrived in New York on 12 September 1815 *with 28 artisans from the south of Ireland*, from Dublin. [SM.77.952]

NEEDHAM, Captain Cheevers, bound from Ireland to Newcastle, Delaware, in 1773. [Penn.Journal;8.9.1773]

NELLY, Captain Houghton, from Cork on 9 November 1790 bound for Dominica. [LL.2244]

NEPTUNE, a brigantine, master Joshua Lawson, from Antigua, British West Indies, to Dublin, 1742. [NRS.GD205.53.8]

NEPTUNE, from Belfast *with passengers* bound for Philadelphia, Pennsylvania, in 1766. [Pa. Journal; 26.6.1766]

NEPTUNE, 70 tons, from Waterford to Newfoundland, 1766-1771. [W401]

NEPTUNE, Captain Carty, from Dublin to Baltimore, Maryland, 13 April 1774. [LL.531]

NEW DRAPER, Captain Wilkinson, from Dublin to Quebec in 1825. [LL.6048]

NEW GRACE, Captain Clark, from Cork bound for Jamaica in 1762. [APCCol.1762.467]

NEW GROVE, Captain Baxter, from Cork on 13 October 1790 bound for New Providence. [LL.2240]

NEW LORD RUSSELL, master .... Hawthorn, bound from Belfast to Guadeloupe, captured by the French and taken to Martinique in 1761. [SM.23.446]

NEW PHOENIX, from Kingstown *with passengers* bound for Jamaica, 1839. [Connaught Journal: 16.4.1840]

NEW SHOREHAM, Captain Surnan, from Cork to Jamaica, 13 December 1773. [LL.500]

NEWRY ASSISTANCE, from Cork *with 23 passengers* ound for Philadelphia, in 1769. [Pa. Journal: 19.10.1769]

NEWRY PACKET, from Ireland *with passengers* bound for Philadelphia, in 1768. [Pa. Journal: 26.5.1768]

SHIPS FROM IRELAND TO EARLY AMERICA, 1623-1850, IV

NIAGARA, arrived in Boston, New England, on 5 December 1848 *with passengers* from Cobh, also arrived in New York *with passengers* from Ireland on 26 February 1847, also on 28 April 1851. [IHR.39.156]

NIMROD, Captain Agnew, from Belfast bound for Charleston, wrecked in the Sound of Harris in the Outer Hebrides on 1 January 1830. [LL6497]

NIPKIN OF BARNSTAPLE, Captain Peter Crane, arrived in Kinsale on 9 June 1668 bound for Virginia. [CSPIre.1668]

NOTTINGHAM, master Laurence Bowden, from Cork to Philadelphia, in 1778. [ActsPCCol.1778.362]

OCEAN, Captain Wise, from Waterford to Newfoundland in 1792. [LL.2313]

OCEAN, arrived in Quebec in May 1826 from Belfast. [LL.6131]

OLD HEAD OF KINSALE, master Robert Barker, from Barbados to the Leeward Islands, on 4 January 1679. [TNA.CO1.]

OLIVE BRANCH, Captain Townley, arrived in Jamaica in February 1816 from Belfast. [LL.6164]

OLIVER OF DUBLIN, master Thomas Atkinson, arrived in Virginia during May 1700. [WI.215]

ORANGE COVE, master Thomas Birch, from Cork bound for Jamaica and Havanna, Cuba, in 1762. [APCCol.1762.467]

SHIPS FROM IRELAND TO EARLY AMERICA, 1623-1850, IV

ORANGE TREE OF NORTH YARMOUTH, 150 tons, Captain Burton, arrived in Kinsale on 16 September 1669 from Barbados bound for Holland. [CSPI]

ORIENT OF NEWCASTLE, arrived at St Peter's Island, Newfoundland, bound for Quebec in 1823 from Dublin. [LL.5841]

ORMOND OF DUBLIN, a frigate, master Henry Brann, arrived in Kinsale on 9 August 1669 from Barbados bound for London. [CSPI]

OXFORD, Captain McLean, from Dublin bound for Maryland in 1766. [LL.3136]

PACIFIC, Captain McDowell, arrived in Quebec in May 1826 from Belfast. [LL.6131]

PACIFIC, Captain Driscoll, arrived in Quebec in May 1826 from Cork. [LL.6131]

PARAGON, Captain Reed, arrived in Trinidad on 1819 from Belfast. [LL.5383]

PARIS, master .... Moore, arrived in Cork from St Andrews, Newfoundland, in 1825. [LL.5974]

PATIENCE, arrived in Quebec in July 1822 from Belfast. [LL.5726]

PATTIE, a brig. from Cork *with passengers* bound for Pennsylvania in 1773. [PaGaz: 24.11.1773]

PEGGY, Captain Howell, from Cork to Jamaica in 1766. [LL.3169]

PEGGY, a brig, master Charles McKinsey, from Belfast *with passengers* bound for Philadelphia, Pennsylvania, arrived on 17 June 1773.

SHIPS FROM IRELAND TO EARLY AMERICA, 1623-1850, IV

PEGGY, Captain Cornwall, from Cork to Rhode Island in 1774. [LL.551]

PEGGY, Captain Manrig, from Youghal *with passengers* bound for Newfoundland in May 1780. [FLJ.24-27 May 1780]

PEGGY, a 200 ton brig, master George Stewart, from Londonderry to Newcastle and Philadelphia, Pennsylvania, in March 1784. [LJ; 13.1.1784]

PEGGY, Captain Brenock, from Waterford to Newfoundland in 1805. [LL.4233]

PENELOPE, Captain Stanton, from Dublin on 16 September 1784 bound for Antigua. [LL.1606]

PENN, a snow, Captain McCaine, from Cork bound for St Kitts on 5 February 1772. [LL.3752]; master J. McCadden, from Cork *with passengers* bound for Philadelphia, arrived 11 July 1773.

PETER AND PAUL, master .... Wight, from Cork bound for St Kitts, British West Indies, in 1758, was captured by the French and taken to Martinique. [SM.21.157]

PETERSFIELD, Captain Lawrence, from Cork to Jamaica, 21 December 1773. [LL.499]

PHEBE, Captain Matthews, from Cork to Grenada on 7 January 1766. [LL.3131]

PHILADELPHIA, master James Malcolm, from Belfast *with passengers* bound for Newcastle, Delaware, and Philadelphia, arrived 22 August 1772.

PHILIP OF WATERFORD, master Richard Curtis, arrived in Funchal, Madeira, in December 1774 from Cork. [ARM.ms699]

PHILLIS, from Baltimore, Maryland, to Belfast in 1771; returned to Baltimore in September 1771. [BNL]

PHOEBE, master John Atkinson, from Waterford bound for Jamaica, 1762. [APCCol.1762.467]

PHOEBE, master .... Dennis, from Cork to Dominica in 1772. [LL.3742]

PHOEBE AND PEGGY, master David McCulloch, from Newry *with passengers* bound for Newcastle, Delaware, and Philadelphia, Pennsylvania, arrived 27 August 1772.

PHOENIX, from Dublin to Philadelphia, Pennsylvania, in 1729. [Dublin Gazette]

PHOENIX, from Baltimore, Maryland, to Belfast in 1771. [BNL]

PHOENIX, Captain Vibert, from Waterford to Newfoundland, 14 April 1774. [LL.531]

PITT, Captain Bailey, from Cork to Philadelphia in 1764. [LL.2976]; Captain Barclay, from Cork to Maryland in 1765. [LL.3135]

PLAIN DEALING, from Kinsale, *with passengers* bound for Jamaica 1656. [IC.ii.898/908/921]

PLANTER, arrived in New Orleans on 3 May 1826 from Belfast. [LL.6121]

POACHER, Captain Malcolm, arrived in New York on 22 April 1819 from Cork. [LL.5387]

POLLY, master .... MacNamara, from Dublin and Madeira in 1758, captured by the French and taken to St Thomas in the West Indies. [SM.21.158/271]

SHIPS FROM IRELAND TO EARLY AMERICA, 1623-1850, IV

POLLY, a brig, from Belfast *with passengers* bound for Philadelphia, Pennsylvania, in 1771. [PaGaz: 6.2.1772]

POER ANTONIO, Captain McCulloch, from Cork to Jamaica, 26 December 1773. [LL.500]

PORTLAND, Captain Bramwell, from Waterford to Grenada in 1774. [LL.551]

POTTY, Captain Knighton, from Cork to Newfoundland, 11 April 1774. [LL.531]

PRESTON, master John Crowther, from Plymouth and Cork bound for Barbados, Carolina, and Virginia in 1698. [TNA.HCA.Exams.Vol.81.April 1700]

PRINCE EDWARD, master William James Wallace, from Cork bound for Martinique and Guadaloupe, French West Indies, in 1762. [APC.Col.1762.467]

PRINCE FREDERICK OF WHITEHAVEN, master John Lutwidge, from Dublin *with passengers* bound for 'the West Indies and other places before her return home', in 1729. [FDJ.14.6.1729][Dublin Gazette]

PRINCE GEORGE, Captain Campbell, from Dublin to Jamaica in 1775. [LL.658]

PRINCE OF ORANGE, master Thomas Dunbar, from Waterford bound for Martinique and Guadeloupe, French West Indies, in 1762. [APCCol.1762.467]

PRINCE OF THE ASTORIAS, Captain Morris, from Dublin to Quebec in 1825. [LL.6055]; arrived in Quebec in May 1826 from Dublin. [LL.6131]

PRINCE OF WALES, master .....Cooke, from Dublin bound for Monte Christi, Hispaniola, captured by the

French and taken to Martinique, French West Indies, in 1761. [SM.23.615]; Captain Egger, from Belfast to South Carolina in 1766. [LL.3164]

PRINCE OF WALES, Captain Patterson, from Cork to St Kitts in 1766. [LL.3169]

PRINCE OF WALES, master Jeremy Bett, at Funchal, Madeira, in October 1793 when bound from Cork to the West Indies. [ARM.ms699]

PRINCE OF WALES, Captain Campbell, from Cork to Jamaica in 1803. [LL.4349]

PRINCE OF WALES, arrived in Miramachi, New Brunswick, on 18 August 1823 from Ireland. [LL.5841]

PRINCE WILLIAM, Captain Hindman, from Cork bound for St Kitts, was captured by the French and taken to Morlaix in France in 1757. [SM.19.556]

PRINCETON, arrived in New York *with passengers* from Ireland on 31 January 1849; also, on 20 September 1849, 19 April 1850, 14 August 1850, 1 November 1850, 3 March 1851, 27 October 1851, 3 March 1852, 11 June 1852, 25 September 1852, 18 July 1853, 26 February 1854, 24 October 1854. [IHR.39.156]

PRISCILLA, master ..... Harris, from Newfoundland to Waterford in 1772. [LL.3742]

PROSPERITY, from Carrickfergus *with passengers* bound for Philadelphia, Pennsylvania, in 1729. [PaGaz]

PROVIDENCE OF KINSALE, arrived in Kinsale on 16 September 1669 from Antigua and Montserrat, in the British West Indies. [CSPI]

SHIPS FROM IRELAND TO EARLY AMERICA, 1623-1850, IV

PROVIDENCE OF DUBLIN, arrived in Virginia by 1699. [WI.193]

PROVIDENCE, a 50 ton pink, master Charles Hunt, via Londonderry bound for Barbados, 1702. [APCCol.1702.860]

PROVIDENCE OF BRISTOL, master.... Tedball, from Cork bound for Jamaica in 1758, captured by the French. [SM.20.219]

PROVIDENCE, Captain Aghorn, arrived in Dominica in 1774 from Cork. [LL.530]

PROVIDENCE, Captain Marshall, from Waterford to Newfoundland, 14 April 1774. [LL.531]

PROVIDENCE, Captain Bailey, arrived in Newfoundland on 19 May 1826 from Waterford. [LL.6121]

PRUSSIAN HERO, master Thomas Quirk, from Cork bound for Jamaica and Havana, Cuba, in 1762. [APCCol.1762.467]

PURCELL, master ..... Carr, from Cork to Antigua in 1772. [LL.3742]

QUEBEC TRADER, arrived in Quebec in May 1826 from Dublin. [LL.6131]

QUEEN CHARLOTTE, a brigantine, master James McClelland, at Funchal, Madeira, on 11 October 1793 when bound from Cork to Dominica. [ARM.ms699]

QUEEN OF THE WEST, arrived in New York *with passengers* from Ireland on 5 April 1849. [IHR.39.156]

SHIPS FROM IRELAND TO EARLY AMERICA, 1623-1850, IV

RACHEL, Captain Duff, from Limerick to New York in 1790. [LL.2226]

RAMBLER, Captain Baxter, from Dublin to Quebec in 1825. [LL.6051]

RAWLINSON, master Moses Benson, from Cork bound for the Leeward Islands, British West Indies, in 1762. [APCCol.1762.467]

RAWLINSON, Captain Hart, from Cork on 9 November 1790 bound for Dominica. [LL.2244]

REBECCA, Captain Bradley, from Cork to St Kitts on 6 September 1790. [LL.2238]; Captain Masters, from Cork to Dominica in 1792. [LL.2317]

REBECCA AND CATHERINE, master Bartholemew Sennet, from Bristol, England, and Cork bound for Antigua, 1762. [APCCol.1762.467]

RECOVERY, master ..... Stephenson, from Londonderry bound for Philadelphia, Pennsylvania, in 1758, captured by the French but ransomed. [SM.20.498]

RECOVERY, 100 tons, Captain Stephen Forrestal, from Waterford to Newfoundland, *with passengers,* 1769. [W378/401]

RECOVERY, a galley, master Matthew Lewtar, at Funchal, Madeira, 11 January 1793 when bound from Cork to Jamaica. [ARM.699]

RECOVERY, from Dublin to Antigua in 1803. [LL.4343]

RELIEF, Captain Martin, arrived in St John, New Brunswick, on 18 May 1826 from Belfast. [LL.6121]

RESOLUTION, arrived in Quebec on 23 June 1823 from Belfast. [LL.6284]

REVOLUTION, Captain Burk, from New York to Waterford in 1793. [LL.2469]

REYNOLDS, Captain Nunns, from Cork to Grenada, 14 December 1773. [LL.500]

RHODERIC DHU, arrived in New York *with passengers* from Ireland on 6 January 1852. [IHR.39.156]

RICHARD WATSON, a brig, *with passengers,* arrived in Quebec on 8 November 1847.

RISBOROUGH, Captain Cassie, arrived in Antigua in February 1826 bound for Jamaica from Ireland. [LL.6103]

ROB ROY, arrived in Quebec in May 1826 from Belfast. [LL.6131]

ROBERT OF BRISTOL, from Kinsale to Barbados on 11 October 1667. [CSPIre.1667]

ROBERT OF KINSALE, arrived in Kinsale in September 1667 from Barbados. [CSPIre.1667]

ROBERT, master ...... Shannon, from Cork bound for St Kitts, captured by the French and taken to Martinique, French West Indies, in 1756. [SM.18.626]

ROBERT, Captain Fowks, from Cork in January 1772 bound for Barbados. [LL.3749]

ROBERT AND FRANCIS, 200 tons, master John Burroughs, via Ireland bound for Jamaica, 1702. [APCCol.1702.860]

SHIPS FROM IRELAND TO EARLY AMERICA, 1623-1850, IV

ROBERT AND MARY, Captain Conolly, from Waterford to Newfoundland, 1766 and 1771. [W401]

ROBERT KERR, Captain Boyd, arrived in Charleston, South Carolina, on 20 February 1826 from Waterford. [LL.6104]

ROSCIUS, arrived in New York *with passengers* from Ireland on 7 March 1849. [IHR.39.156]

ROSE, master Robert George, from Londonderry *with passengers* bound for Newcastle, Delaware, and Philadelphia, Pennsylvania, arrived 23 July 1772; master Robert George, from Londonderry *with passengers* bound for Newcastle, Delaware, and Philadelphia, arrived 23 July 1773; master Joseph Curry, from Londonderry *with passengers* bound for Baltimore, Maryland, in 1775. [PaGaz: 8.1776]

ROSE, Captain Morse, from Cork to Jamaica, 14 December 1773. [LL.500]

ROSE, Captain Curry, arrived in Londonderry from New York in March 1775. [BEP:4.3.1775]

ROSE, Captain Lee, arrived in Quebec on 11 July 1822 from Belfast. [LL.5728]

ROSS, Captain Christopher, from Newfoundland to Waterford in 1772. [LL.3742]

ROYAL CHARLOTTE, Captain Harrison, from Cork to Dominica in 1766. [LL.3169]

ROYAL DUKE, master Michael Tovey, from Cork bound for the West Indies, 1762. [APCCol.1762.467]

ROYAL EAGLE, Captain Black, from Limerick to Jamaica in 1825. [LL.6049]

SHIPS FROM IRELAND TO EARLY AMERICA, 1623-1850, IV

ROYAL EXCHANGE, Captain Martin, from Cork to Antigua in 1766. [LL.3165]

ROYAL GEORGE, Captain Grant, arrived in Quebec in May 1826 from Dublin. [LL.6131]

RUBY OF LIVERPOOL, from Dublin to Antigua in March 1740. [Dublin News-letter 7.3.1740]

RUBY, Captain Cook, from Cork to Dominica in 1775. [LL.666]

RUBY OF WATERFORD, arrived in Quebec in May 1826 from Waterford. [LL.6131]

RUMBO, a 180 ton galley, bound via Ireland for Barbados and the Leeward Islands, in 1704. [APCCol.1705.915/916]

SAINT ANDREW, arrived in Martinique on 6 January 1745 from Cork. [PRONI.D2707.A1.9.6]

SAINT ANDREW, master James Hutchison, from Belfast to Kingston, Jamaica, in 1755. [PRONI.D354.576]

SAINT ANN OF GALWAY, arrived in Kinsale on 15 July 1669 from Barbados bound for London. [CSP I]

SAINT GEORGE, Captain Lord, arrived in Kinsale in June 1667 bound for the West Indies. [CSPIre.1667]

SAINT GEORGE, Captain Palmer, arrived in Jamaica in May 1803 from Cork. [LL.4362]

SAINT GEORGE, arrived in New York *with passengers* from Ireland on 21 August 1848. [IHR.39.156]

SAINT JAMES, master Malachi Foot, from Cork bound for the West Indies, 1762. [APCCol.1762.467]

SHIPS FROM IRELAND TO EARLY AMERICA, 1623-1850, IV

SAINT JAMES, master Mark Collins, from Belfast *with 270 passengers* bound for Newcastle, Delaware, arrived in July 1789. [Pennsylvania Packet: 25.7.1789]

SAINT JOHN OF DUBLIN, master Peter Lawrence, seized by the Customs Collector of New England, 1680. [SPAWI.1680.1625]

SAINT MARY'S PLANTER, Captain Gill, from Cork to Grenada in 1774. [LL.573]

SAINT MICHAEL, Captain Aylward, from Waterford to the West Indies 1766-1771. [W401]

SAINT PATRICK, master ..... Sarsfield, from Cork bound for Jamaica in 1758, captured by the French. [SM.20.219]

SAINT PATRICK, Captain Jones, arrived in Newfoundland on 23 August 1823 from Belfast. [LL.5841]

SAINT PETER OF PLYMOUTH, from Galway to Barbados, 1666. [ActsPCCol.723]

SAINT PETER, master Thomas Smith, bound from Liverpool and Cork for Jamaica, 1762. [APCCol.1762.467]

SAINT PETER, Captain Barbe, from Cork to Newfoundland, 7 April 1774. [LL.529]

SAINT THOMAS, Captain Kennedy, from Waterford to Newfoundland, 1766-1771. [W402]

SAINT JOHN OF DUBLIN, master Peter Lawrence, seized by the Customs Collector of New England, 1680. [SPAWI.1680.1625]

SHIPS FROM IRELAND TO EARLY AMERICA, 1623-1850, IV

SAINT JOHN OF DUBLIN, master Peter Lawrence, seized by the Customs Collector of New England, 1680. [SPAWI.1680.1625]

SAINT MARY'S PLANTER, Captain Gill. From Cork to Grenada in 1774. [LL.573]

SALLY, master .... Nichols, from Belfast bound for Antigua in 1757, captured by the French. [SM.20.109]

SALLY, master ...... Taylor, from Cork bound for Guadeloupe, captured by the French and taken to Martinique, in 1759. [SM.22.49]

SALLY, master William Floyd, from Cork bound for Martinique and St Kitts, British West Indies, in 1762. [APCCol.1762.467]

SALLY, Captain Afman, from Cork to Jamaica in 1775. [LL.666]

SALLY, master Richard Curtis, from Waterford *with passengers* bound for Philadelphia, Pennsylvania, arrived there on 7 July 1772; from Cork *with 21 passengers* bound for Philadelphia in 1773. [Pa.Journal: 27.10.1773]; Captain Russell, from Cork bound for Philadelphia in 1775. [LL.666]

SALLY, Captain Williams, from Londonderry to Baltimore, Maryland, in 1803. [LL.4313]

SALLY, Captain Art, from Belfast to Philadelphia, Pennsylvania, in 1803. [LL.4313]

SALLY, Captain Mitchell, arrived in the Gulf of the St Lawrence on 18 July 1817 from Belfast. [LL.5202]

SALLY, Captain Mitchelson, from Dublin to Barbados in 1819. [LL.5384]

SALLY, master Richard Curtis, from Waterford *with passengers* bound for Philadelphia, Pennsylvania, arrived there on 7 July 1772; from Cork *with 21 passengers* bound for Philadelphia in 1773. [PaJournal: 27.10.1773]; Captain Russell, from Cork bound for Philadelphia in 1775. [LL.666]

SALLY, Captain Williams, from Londonderry to Baltimore, Maryland, in 1803. [LL.4313]

SAM LAWRENCE, arrived in New York *with passengers* from Ireland on 21 September 1852. [IHR.39.156]

SAMOSET, Captain Rich, arrived in Charleston, South Carolina, on 18 February 1826 from Belfast. [LL.6104]

SAMUEL OF DUBLIN, from Dublin to Barbados in March 1740. [Dublin News-letter 7.3.1740]

SAMUEL, Captain Johnson, from Dublin bound for Philadelphia in 1766. [LL.3138]

SAMUEL AND MARY, 150 tons, Captain Simons, from Waterford to Philadelphia, between 1766 and 1771. [W402]

SAN DOMINGO, Captain Lewis, arrived in Prince Edward Island on 30 June 1822 from Waterford. [LL.5728]

SARA AND ABIGAIL, from Cork to Port Royal, Jamaica, 1688. [TNA.CO142.13]

SARAH, a snow, master Samuel Corry, from Dublin *with passengers* bound for Newcastle, Delaware, and Philadelphia, Pennsylvania, arrived there on 1 September 1773.

SARAH, Captain Cleaton, from Cork to Jamaica, 20 December 1773. [LL.499]

SHIPS FROM IRELAND TO EARLY AMERICA, 1623-1850, IV

SARAH, from Limerick *with passengers* bound for Canada, illegally landed passengers on Prince Edward Island in 1817. [PROI.CE.bundle 1a-3a-2, number 53]

SARAH, from Sligo with passengers bound for America on 10 May 1849. [Ballina Chronicle: 16.5.1849]

SARAH ELIZABETH, arrived in Quebec in July 1822 from Limerick. [LL.5726]

SARAH G. HYDE, arrived in New York *with passengers* from Ireland on 5 December 1846. [IHR.39.156]

SATISFACTION, Captain Woodhouse, from Cork to America in 1799. [LL.3067]

SCHUYKILL, Captain Nicolls, from Cork to New York in 1825. [LL.6048]

SCIPIO, Captain Beadle, arrived in Newfoundland on 2 July 1823 from Waterford. [LL.5284]

SCOURFIELD, Captain Ritvy, arrived in Jamaica in May 1826 from Cork. [LL.6129]

SEA, arrived in New York *with passengers* from Ireland on 4 June 1849. [IHR.39.156]

SEAFLOWER OF BRISTOL, arrived in Kinsale on 18 November 1667 from Barbados. [CSPIre.1667]

SEAFLOWER OF JAMAICA, arrived in Dunfanaghy on 20 June 1696. [APCCol.VI.vii]

SEAFLOWER, from Belfast *with 106 passengers,* bound for Philadelphia on 31 July 1741, arrived in Boston, New England, on 31 October *with 43 passengers.*

SEA NYMPH, arrived in New York *with passengers* from Ireland on 24 July 1854. [IHR.39.156]

SEBASTIAN, Captain White, from Belfast on 25 September 1790 bound for Antigua. [LL.2234]

SERVANNA OF GALWAY, when in Barbados was impressed into government service, a petition by Lawrence Deane in 1667. [PCCol.1667.706]

SHANNON, arrived in New York *with passengers* from Ireland on 10 July 1851. [IHR.39.156]

SHELLET, Captain Mason, from Waterford to Quebec in 1825. [LL.6048]

SIDDONS, arrived in New York *with passengers* from Ireland on 19 September 1854. [IHR.39.156]

SIR T. DUCKWORTH, arrived in Jamaica in 1819 from Cork. [LL.5385]

SIR WATKIN, arrived in Quebec in May 1826 from Belfast. [LL.6131]

SISTERS, Captain Kent, arrived in Newfoundland in June 1823 from Waterford. [LL.5823]

SIZARGH, from northern Ireland *with passengers* bound for America in 1721. [American Weekly Mercury: 17 August 1721]

SOCIETY OF DUBLIN, master ... Fitzgerald, scheduled to sail from Flushing, Zealand, to Bilbao, Spain, the Canaries, the Spanish West Indies, and then to England, however in Bilbao .... Parks was appointed master and the ship returned to Cork, then it sailed for Philadelphia bound for Carthagena. The ship landed at Petit Guaves and returned to the Delaware, before July 1712. [ActsPCCol.IV. 244]

SHIPS FROM IRELAND TO EARLY AMERICA, 1623-1850, IV

SPEEDWELL, 70 tons, master Robert Hatch, from Dartmouth, England, via Ireland bound for Newfoundland, in 1702. [APCCol.1702.860]

SPEEDWELL, master ... Stewart, from Dublin bound for Antigua, captured by the French in 1758 and taken to Guadeloupe, also in 1761. [SM.21.50; 23.221]

SPEEDWELL, Captain Jones, from Waterford to Philadelphia in 1774. [LL.573]

SPENCER, Captain Groves, from Cork to Jamaica, 21 December 1773. [LL.499]

SPRIGHTLY, arrived in Quebec in July 1822 from Belfast. [LL.5726]; arrived in Quebec on 4 August 1823. [LL.5836]

STAR OF THE WEST, arrived in New York *with passengers* from Ireland on 13 July 1853. [IHR.39.156]

SUBMISSION OF BRISTOL, master John Smith, arrived in Kinsale in June 1667 from Barbados. [CSPIre.]

SUCCESS, master ..... Dunn, from Philadelphia, to Cork in 1758, was captured by the French and burnt. [SM.20.611]

SUCCESS, master .... Daly, bound from Kinsale for Quiberon Bay, France, captured by the French and taken to Port Louis, Grenada, in 1760. [SM.23.53]

SUCCESS, master Joseph Cookson, bound from Bristol, England, and Cork for the West Indies, in 1762. [APCCol.1762.467]

SHIPS FROM IRELAND TO EARLY AMERICA, 1623-1850, IV

SUCCESS, Captain James GILL, from Waterford *with 80 passengers* bound for Harbour Grace, Newfoundland, in 1767. [W.383]

SUCCESS, a brigantine, master Duncan Niven, at Funchal, Madeira, on 11 October 1793 when bound from Belfast to St Vincent, British West Indies. [ARM.ms699]

SUNTON OF WHITEHAVEN, Captain Burton, from St Andrews, New Brunswick, bound for Sligo, was wrecked off the Isle of Skye, Scotland on 30 November 1818. [LL.5343]

SUSAN, master .... Hepburn, from Cork bound for Antigua in 1759, captured by the French and taken to St Domingo, French West Indies. [SM.21.109]

SUSAN, Captain O'Connor, arrived in New York on 17 June 1804 from Ireland. [Maryland Gazette #2995]

SUSANNA, Captain Connor, from Waterford to Halifax, Nova Scotia in 1765. [LL.3128]

SUSANNAH, Captain Conklin, arrived in New York in June 1803 from Dublin, [LL.4367]; Captain Collins, from Dublin to New York in 1805. [LL.4225]

SUSPENSE, Captain Crowley, arrived in St John, New Brunswick, on 18 May 1826 from Dublin. [LL.6121]

SUSQUEHANNAH, Captain Stewart, arrived in New York on 25 June 1823 from Sligo. [LL.5825]

SWALLOW, a brig, from Waterford *with 23 passengers* bound for Philadelphia, Pennsylvania, in 1769. [Pa.Journal.] [PRONI.D1044.176]; from Waterford *with 23 passengers* bound for Philadelphia in 1773. [Pa.Journal:25.8.1773]; from Waterford to Newfoundland in 1792. [LL.2317]

SHIPS FROM IRELAND TO EARLY AMERICA, 1623-1850, IV

SWALLOW, Captain McClea, from Cork to St Augustine, Florida, on 14 April 1774. [LL.531]

SWIFT, master .... Strange, from Cork bound for Antigua in 1757, captured by the French. [SM.20.109]

SWIFT, Captain Clark, from Cork to New York in 1805, [LL.4227]

TARBOLTON, Captain Carswell, from Londonderry *with passengers* bound for Quebec in 1836. [LJ.16.8.1836]

TARTAR, master Michael Nowlan, from Cork bound for Martinique, 1762. [APCCol.1762.467]

THARTUS, arrived in New York *with passengers* from Ireland on 18 November 1847. [IHR.39.156]

THETIS, Captain Moncur, from Cork to Jamaica, on 13 December 1773. [LL.500]

THISTLE, Captain Dunley, arrived in Newfoundland on 20 August 1823 from Belfast. [LL.5841]

THOMAS, a brig, from New York to Ireland in 1732.

THOMAS, Captain Laird, from Cork to Jamaica on 7 January 1766. [LL.3131]

THOMAS OF DUBLIN, a brig, master .... Stewart, when returning from Barbados to Dublin was wrecked off Cork on 5 September 1766.

THOMAS, Captain Coveyduck, from Youghal *with passengers* bound for Newfoundland in May 1780. [FLJ.24-27 May 1780]

SHIPS FROM IRELAND TO EARLY AMERICA, 1623-1850, IV

THOMAS, Captain Gelston, arrived in Philadelphia, Pennsylvania, in 1817 from Belfast. [LL.5185]

THOMAS, Captain Battersby, arrived in Quebec in May 1826 from Belfast. [LL.6131]

THOMAS, Captain Wareham, arrived in Quebec in May 1826 from Dublin. [LL.6131]

THOMAS AND SAMUEL, master Daniel Browne, via Ireland bound for Barbados, 1702. [APCCol.1702.860]

THOMAS TYSON, arrived in Barbados on 18 April 1817 from Dublin. [LL.5183]

THREE FRIENDS, master Crannel, from Waterford bound for New York, captured by the French and taken to Corunna, Spain, in 1760. [SM.23.165]; master .... Cherry, from Waterford bound for America in 1761 was captured by the French and taken to Bayonne, France. [SM.23.557]

THREE FRIENDS, master .... Hutchins, from Cork to St Eustatia, Dutch West Indies, in 1772. [LL.3744]

THREE JOHNS, a ketch, from Dublin bound for Montserrat around 1695. [TNA.HCA.Exams.Vol.53.1702]

THREE SISTERS, Captain Hudson, from Dublin to Antigua in 1766. [LL.3165]

TIBBIE, Captain Andrews, from Glasgow via Belfast bound for Barbados and the Leeward Islands, captured by the French but ransomed in 1760. [SM.22.335/502]

TIBER, arrived in Quebec in July 1822 from Dublin. [LL.5726]

SHIPS FROM IRELAND TO EARLY AMERICA, 1623-1850, IV

TIFFIN, Captain Dryden, arrived in New York on 5 June 1817 from Dublin. [LL.6192]

TIGER, Captain Hawkins, from Waterford to Newfoundland in 1817. [LL.5185]

TOM, Captain Brown, arrived in Georgetown, South Carolina, on 18 December 1818 from Belfast. [LL.5352]

TORTULA PACKET, Captain Norris, from Cork to Barbados on 14 January 1766. [LL.3127]

TOTTENHAM, Captain Kees, arrived in Quebec in May 1826 from Ross. [LL.6131]

TRAFALGAR, Captain Christopherson, arrived in Quebec in May 1826 from Waterford. [LL.6131]

TRIAL, 70 tons, Captain Byrne, from Waterford to Philadelphia and the West Indies, between 1766 and 1771. [W402]

TRIDENT, Captain Towes, arrived in Philadelphia on 20 July 1822 from Belfast, [LL.5727]; Captain Coffin, from Londonderry to New York in 1825. [LL.6056]; from Belfast to New York, arrived in May 1826. [LL.2114]

TRITON, Captain Saunders, from Cork on 22 June 1764 bound for Newfoundland. [LL.2972]

TRITON, Captain Wilkison, arrived in New York on 11 July 1823 from Londonderry. [LL.5828]

TRUMAN, Captain Shepherd, from Cork to St Eustatia, Dutch West Indies, in 1774. [LL.529]

TRUMBULL, arrived in New York *with passengers* from Ireland on 23 May 1851. [IHR.39.156]

TWO BROTHERS, master .... Jenner, from Dublin bound for Jamaica, captured by the French and taken to Puerto Rico in 1759. [SM.21.443]; Captain Allen, from New York to Newry in 1766. [LL.3165]

TWO BROTHERS, Captain Keogh, from Waterford to Newfoundland, 14 April 1774. [LL.531]

TWO FRIENDS, Captain McClean, from Cork to Jamaica on 3 January 1766. [LL.3130]

TWO FRIENDS, Captain Latham, from Belfast to New York in 1805. [LL.4227]

TWO MARYS, Captain Tilyou, from Belfast to Boston, New England, in 1825. [LL.5974]

TYGER, master ... Storey, from Cork to Jamaica in 1772. [LL.3743]

TYGRESS, master ..... Byem, from Dublin bound for Montserrat, British West Indies, in 1758, captured by the French and taken to Guadeloupe, French West Indies. [SM.20.330]

UNION, Captain Semple, from Boston bound for Dublin, wrecked in the Sound of Mull, Scotland, on 9 February 1787. [LL.1859]

UNION, Captain Crisewell, arrived in Dingle from Philadelphia, Pennsylvania, in 1793. [LL.2467]

UNION, master J. Landy, arrived in Prince Edward Island from Cork on 6 August 1793. [PAPEI.RG9]

UNION, Captain Murphy, arrived in St Vincent in May 1803 from Cork. [LL.4361]

SHIPS FROM IRELAND TO EARLY AMERICA, 1623-1850, IV

UNITY, master Jacob Moulson, from Dublin via Barbados to Virginia in 1654.

UNITY, master .... Elinor, from Cork bound for St Eustatia, Dutch West Indies, captured by the French and taken to Martinique in 1757. [SM.19.325]

VALENTINE, 100 tons, Captain Nowlan, from Waterford to Newfoundland, between 1766 and 1771. [W402]

VALENTINE, Captain Scallion, from Dublin to Antigua in 1805. [LL.4224]

VALIANT, Captain Baffam, arrived in Cork from Salem, New England, in 1793. [LL.2467]

VERONICA, arrived in Charleston, South Carolina, on 25 April 1826 from Belfast. [LL.6122]

VESTA, arrived in New York *with passengers* from Ireland on 9 April 1851. [IHR.39.156]

VICTORIA, Captain McKenna, arrived in Quebec on 27 June 1817 from Dublin. [LL.5201]

VIGILANT, master Richard Ayre, at Funchal, Madeira, 29 August 1806, when bound from Cork to Jamaica, *with 4 passengers.* [ARM.ms600]

VINE OF DUBLIN, *with passengers*, arrived in Virginia by 1693. [WI.195]

VINE, Captain Hunter, from Dublin to Quebec in 1825. [LL.6048]

VIRGINIA, arrived in New York on 12 September 1815 *with 20 passengers, natives of Tipperary,* from Waterford. [SM.77.952]

VIRGINIAN, arrived in New York *with passengers* from Ireland on 15 May 1846. [IHR.39.156]

VOLUNTEER, Captain Wilkinson, from Cork to Jamaica in 1803. [LL.4349]; Captain Bell, arrived in Quebec in May 1826 from Cork. [LL.6121]

WADDELL, Captain Scott, from Belfast to Maryland in March 1775. [BEP:4.3.1775]

WALLER, a brig, Captain Hannay, from Dublin to Barbados in January 1816. [SNL: 9.1.1816]

WALLSEND, Captain Ramsay, arrived in Quebec in May 1826 from Cork. [LL.6131]

WADDELL, Captain Scott, from Belfast to Maryland in March 1775. [BEP:4.3.1775]

WALWORTH, master Edward Boggs, from Cork *with passengers* bound for Philadelphia in 1767, [PaJournal:8.10.1767]; master C. McCausland, from Londonderry *with passengers* bound for Newcastle, Delaware, and Philadelphia, arrived 7 September 1772.

WARREN'S TOWN, Captain Sullivan, from Cork on 10 September 1783 bound for Halifax, Nova Scotia. [LL.1605]

WARWICK, from London via Cork bound for Jamaica, 1762. [APCCol.1762.467]

WELLINGTON, Captain Pudey, arrived in St Vincent on 15 February 1819 from Cork, [LL.5383]; Captain Keller, arrived in Jamaica on 15 February 1826 from Cork. [LL.6104]

SHIPS FROM IRELAND TO EARLY AMERICA, 1623-1850, IV

WENSBECK, arrived in Quebec in May 1826 from Cork. [LL.6131]

WESTERN EMPIRE, arrived in New York *with passengers* from Ireland on 21 November 1854. [IHR.39.156]

WESTERN WORLD, arrived in New York *with passengers* from Ireland on 13 October 1851. [IHR.39.156]

WHIG, master ..... Hamilton, from Londonderry bound for Antigua, captured by the French and taken to Vigo, Spain, in 1759. [SM.21.387]

WHITBY, Captain Scott, from Waterford in 1822 bound for Quebec. [LL.5726]

WHITE HORSE OF LONDON, from Kinsale to Barbados on 11 October 1667. [CSPIre.1667]

WILLIAM, Captain Power, from Waterford to Newfoundland, 1766-1771. [W402]

WILLIAM, Captain Emmeter, from Youghal *with passengers* bound for Newfoundland in May 1780. [FLJ.24-27 May 1780]

WILLIAM, a brigantine, master William Barry, at Funchal, Madeira, 3 February 1793 when bound from Cork to St Vincent, at Funchal, Madeira, 10 March 1795 when bound from Cork to the West Indies. [ARM.mss698/699]

WILLIAM, Captain Penn, from Dublin to Quebec in 1825. [LL.6055]; arrived in Quebec in May 1826 from Dublin. [LL.6131]

WILLIAM, from Belfast to Quebec in 1825. [LL.6055]

WILLIAM, Captain Fell, arrived in Quebec in May 1826 from Newry. [LL.6131]

WILLIAM AND GEORGE OF BALLYCASTLE, from Portrush to America in 1754 *with passengers.*

WILLIAM AND JAMES, Captain Bell, from Belfast on 2 October 1790 bound for Jamaica. [LL.2237]

WILLIAM AND JAMES, a galley, master George Hunt, at Funchal, Madeira, 28 November 1794, when bound from Waterford to Jamaica. [ARM.ms699]

WILLIAM D. SEWELL, arrived in New York *with passengers* from Ireland on 4 September 1850, also on 15 October 1852, 4 May 1853. [IHR.39.156]

WILMINGTON, Captain Woodward, from Belfast to Philadelphia, Pennsylvania, in 1803. [LL.4343]

WILSON, Captain Thornton, bound from Cork for Jamaica, in 1762. [APCCol.1762.467]

WILTSHIRE, a galley, master Jacob Hollister, from Bristol, England, via Waterford bound for Virginia in 1711. [TNA.E190.1169.1]

WILLIAM WIRT, arrived in New York *with passengers* from Ireland on 28 February 1851. [IHR.39.156]

WOODLAND CASTLE, arrived in Barbados on 1 February 1817 from Cork. [LL.6164]

WOODMAN, Captain Wolfendal, arrived in St John, New Brunswick, on 17 January 1826 from Cork. [LL.6079]

XENOPHON, Captain Elly, arrived in St John, New Brunswick, in July 1822 from Belfast. [LL.2029]

YOUNG CHARLES, Captain Brown, from Cork to Jamaica on 3 January 1766. [LL.3130]

YOUNG JAMES, Captain Bass, from Dublin bound for Antigua, captured by the French and taken to Martinique or Guadeloupe in 1757. [SM.19.493]

YOUNG JENNY, Captain Day, from Youghal *with passengers* bound for Newfoundland in May 1780. [FLJ.24-27 May 1780]

ZACHARY BAILEY, Captain Hodge, from Cork to Jamaica, 13 December 1773. [LL.500]

ZEEMAN, Captain Simons, from Cork on 14 December 1783 bound for St Thomas. [LL.1429]

ADDENDUM

.... of Flushing, at Kinsale in October 1667 bound for the Leeward Islands. [CSPIre.1667]

.... of Bristol, at Kinsale in October 1667 bound for Barbados. [CSPIre.1667]

........., a brig, master ..... Trance, from Cork, captured by the French and taken to Guadeloupe in 1756. [SM.18.626]

........., master .... Lewis, from Cork bound for Jamaica, captured by the French and taken to Guadeloupe in 1756. [SM.18.626]

........., master .... Herne, from Cork bound for Jamaica, captured by the French and taken to Guadeloupe in 1756. [SM.18.626]

SHIPS FROM IRELAND TO EARLY AMERICA, 1623-1850, IV

........, master ...... Nicholson, from Cork, captured by the French and taken to Martinique in 1757. [SM.21.109]

........, master .... MacCulloch, from Belfast bound for New York, was captured by the French and taken to Bayonne, France, in 1757. [SM.19.556]

......., master ...... Strachan, from Ireland, captured by the French and taken to Martinique in 1757. [SM.19.613]

........, master .... Hastie, from Cork, was captured by the French and taken to Guadeloupe, French West Indies, in 1758. [SM.20.611]

.... of Dublin, a snow, master ..... Welch, from Philadelphia, Pennsylvania, bound for Antigua, captured by the French and taken to Martinique, French West Indies, in 1760. [SM.22.611]

........., a Danish ship from Dublin bound for Madeira and St Eustatius, Dutch West Indies, in 1780. [APCCol.IV.997]

..........., master William Williams, at Funchal, Madeira, 26 January 1808, bound from Cork to Piscatiqua, New England, *with six passengers.* [ARM.ms600]

........., Captain Jones, arrived in New York on 12 September 1815 *with 52 natives of Cavan, Tipperary and Drogheda* from Ireland. [SM.77.952]

www.ingramcontent.com/pod-product-compliance
Lightning Source LLC
Chambersburg PA
CBHW071227160426
43196CB00012B/2434